PRESENTED TO

_____

FROM

_____

DATE

_____

A Prayer

FOR EVERY OCCASION

CARRIE MARRS

ZONDERVAN®

ZONDERVAN

A Prayer for Every Occasion

© 2020 by Zondervan

Requests for information should be addressed to:
Zondervan, *3900 Sparks Dr. SE, Grand Rapids, Michigan 49546*

ISBN 9780310455394

Art direction: Jen Showalter
Interior design: Emily Ghattas

Printed in China

20 21 22 23 24 GRI 11 10 9 8 7 6 5 4 3 2

Contents

Introduction

True, whole prayer is nothing but love.
—ST. AUGUSTINE OF HIPPO

*F*or some of us, prayer is one big awkward question mark. *What exactly am I supposed to do?*

Others of us have been around prayer enough that it feels familiar. We know what to expect from others and what's expected of us. But we may be praying in a way that is actually quite different from what Scripture reveals about prayer. Or we might find ourselves in a season when prayer has become an afterthought—or something altogether forgotten. Or perhaps we've settled into a good prayer practice, but we could use some fresh inspiration.

I always think of readings that steer me in the right direction as train tracks. Scripture, liturgy, prayers of God's people—these serve as rails that guide my heart and mind in the way they ought to go. They protect me from wandering off into territory that is worthless or dangerous. They are tools of the Spirit to *move me* in the direction of worship and true life in God, especially when I cannot seem to take a step on my own.

Compiling these entries and spending time reflecting on prayers from Christians throughout the centuries has been *so good* for my soul—wonderfully challenging, edifying, and thought-provoking. I've been astonished at how relatable their words are and comforted by seeing that, for ages, so many people have been wrestling with the same challenges that I wrestle with today.

I always seem to need the reminder that having problems in my life and conflict within myself is normal; this is the standard human condition. The important issue is not *Am I struggling?* but *Am I staying close to God through the struggle? Am I depending on Him and finding ways to worship in the midst of all I'm experiencing?*

Seeing these writers throughout history boldly face themselves, demonstrate striking self-awareness, and then present their open hearts (and whole selves) to the powerful presence of God has changed me.

I've been inspired by their vulnerability and courage.

I've gained wisdom from their insights.

I've found it incredibly helpful to borrow their words to express my heart to God. I've also been motivated to write my own prayers (some of which are included in this book and marked with my initials, C. M.).

I hope you have a similar experience of your own . . . one that nourishes your soul, impresses the love and truth of God deeper into your heart, and guides you into a sweeter life of joyful worship and intimacy with our good Father.

—Carrie Marrs

One

An Invitation

To pray is to listen to the One who calls you . . .
"my beloved child." . . . Let that voice speak to
the center of your being, to your guts, and let
that voice resound in your whole being.

—HENRI NOUWEN

The Father is calling your name.

He wants to pull you closer to His heart and reach you with His immense, never-ending love. He wants to change your experience in His world by having you walk through it in deeper relationship with Him. It's what He has had in mind all along.

God created people as an outpouring of the loving relationship between the Father, Son, and Holy Spirit. He wanted to share His abundance and welcome us into His joy and love. We were made for relationship, for close connection with Him, and for worship.

He reached out to us first; He began the conversation and invited us to respond. He calls us to know Him in all His wonder—to experience His joy and love, His power and goodness, His holiness and grace—and respond in prayer. He calls us to open up our hearts to Him and build an intimate relationship with Him.

This extraordinary access to the King of the heavens was not available to our ancestors. The chasm between His holiness and human frailty was too great; temples, sacrifices, and priests were required in any effort to reach Him.

But God pursued us with His love by becoming human and giving us grace, allowing us to be fully identified with His faithful Son. Through Jesus, we can freely come to God's throne in confidence. Through Jesus, we are adopted into the bursting-with-blessings family of God. The Father treats us as He treats Jesus! He firmly roots us in His fierce love, making us secure in a relationship that is based on His choice to love—not on our efforts.

In this place of abundant love, we get to live a life of prayer.

But we often find ourselves retreating from Him. Some days we just don't believe this big-as-the-sky, too-good-to-be-true love. Other times we're distracted, too focused on immediate tasks to turn to Him. Often, we feel inferior or clumsy with words, uncertain what our prayers "ought" to be.

All the while God is saying, with His arms open wide, "Come."

He's not looking for perfect prayers. He doesn't want to be shut out of our lives, whatever the reason. He wants relationship.

Two

The Purpose of Prayer

The function of prayer is . . . to change the nature
of the one who prays.
—SØREN KIERKEGAARD

Scripture shows us many types of interactions with God. We
see Jacob wrestling with God for hours, and Job overcome
with doubt and bitterness in His presence. We see Moses' fearful
excuses and Jonah's stubborn resistance. Then there are the prayers
of Jesus and Mary, which demonstrate complete trust and obedience, a perfect reflection of the will of God.

Our God is compassionate and kind. He will lead us in learn-
ing how to pray. The key is that He doesn't want us to wait until
we've got it right before we come to Him. It's through our authentic
engagement with Him that He forms us. It's through the intimacy
of prayer that we become like Him. So we should seek Him in His

Word and then simply talk to Him. Through that genuine connection, we'll grow.

We seek Him in His Word because, as we've said, prayer is our response to what He has revealed about Himself, our part in the dialogue He began. The goal is not self-exploration or self-expression; it is knowing Him and relating to Him with honesty and reverence.

John Calvin considered prayer to be "the chief exercise of faith . . . by which we daily receive God's benefits." We get to experience His love and joy. We get to receive His peace and strength. As we allow ourselves to be captivated by Him and open ourselves to Him, He'll become more alive in us and transform us. Our attitude will become hopeful, our desires will reflect His, our actions will show His wisdom. Who we are and what we do will show the fruit of His life in us.

As we persist in prayer, we'll develop a lifestyle of dependence, welcoming God's mighty power to reach every corner of our lives. We'll honor Him with our faith, adoration, and praise, and continually submit ourselves to Him, even when it involves suffering. We'll also have the privilege of carrying out His purposes by praying for His will to be done and helping accomplish it.

And so the purposes of prayer are linked to what God designed us for: helping us to build our relationship with Him, to live in our true identity as worshipers of Him, and to become like Him.

Three

A Guide to Prayer

Each time, before you [pray], be quiet first, and
worship God in His glory. Think of what He can
do, and how He delights to hear the prayers of
His redeemed people. Think of your place and
privilege in Christ, and expect great things!

—ANDREW MURRAY

The disciples had observed Jesus' prayer habits. Why was He
going into the wilderness alone? What was He saying while He
was there? They wanted to start doing whatever He was doing, taking on His practices.

WHAT TO PRAY FOR

When the disciples asked Jesus how to pray, He answered them by giving them a model prayer—*say this, or something like it.* He gave this prayer to us as well so we could not only repeat His very words but also use them as guiding principles, as a jumping-off point for our own prayers. For example:

Our Father in heaven,
> *We are privileged to come to You in the name of Jesus, our mediator and brother.*

May Your name be kept holy.
> *May we honor You in the way we live. May the whole world honor You.*

May Your kingdom come soon.
> *We invite Your reign in every way—in our hearts and in world events. Change our desires and actions. Put a stop to all injustice and suffering.*

May Your will be done on earth, as it is in heaven.
> *We fully surrender to You; have Your way. We want what You want.*

Give us today the food we need,
> *Provide for us and for everyone in the world,*

and forgive us our sins, as we have forgiven those who sin against us.

> *Keep us repentant and merciful. May Your grace permeate our hearts and relationships.*

And don't let us yield to temptation, but rescue us from the evil one.

> *Guide us, protect us, and help us obey.*

For Yours is the kingdom, the power, and the glory forever.

> *No matter what happens, we celebrate that You, our sovereign King, are on the throne. Nothing is beyond Your great power, and Your kingdom of light is the future. May all creation praise You and marvel at Your glory.*

Amen.

In His prayer, Jesus showed us that asking God for what we need expresses our faith in Him; we honor Him by depending on Him. But Jesus also steers us away from offering prayers composed only of our own complaints, wants, and worries; He is leading us into authentic worship and a deeper relationship with God.

German pastor and theologian Dietrich Bonhoeffer wrote, "The richness of the Word of God ought to determine our prayer, not the poverty of our heart." God wants us to open our hearts to Him, to come as we are, but He also wants to lead us to the point where we are praying what He wants us to pray.

He has given us many more examples, beyond Jesus' model prayer, of what to pray for throughout the New Testament:

- greater faith
- more of the Holy Spirit
- forgiveness, grace, peace, comfort—every kind of spiritual blessing and help for the soul
- healing and protection
- spiritual growth—to become mature and holy
- spiritual wisdom for godly living
- guidance in decision making
- strength to fight temptation
- the courage and power to obey
- opportunities to do His work and will
- our concerns and needs as well as others' concerns and needs
- help in bringing others to faith in the gospel
- leaders
- blessings on our enemies

We are to pray in Jesus' name, acknowledging our access to the Father through the Son, and we are to pray in the Spirit, relying on Him to be our helper and guide.

When we feel at a loss in prayer, the Spirit helps us in our weakness (Romans 8:26). We often can't see or grasp what is best, so He prays on our behalf in ways we cannot, praying for what is good for us and will glorify God most. In the meantime, He also increases our hunger for that perfect will of God.

HOW TO PRAY

Jesus pointed out the human tendency to make prayer about us—being seen and respected—and gave practical steps to avoid it.

"When you come before God, don't turn [it] into a theatrical production.... Find a quiet, secluded place so you won't be tempted to role-play before God. Just be there as simply and honestly as you can manage. The focus will shift from you to God, and you will begin to sense his grace. . . . With a God like this loving you, you can pray very simply" (Matthew 6:5–8 THE MESSAGE).

He also said not to babble on, praying long prayers filled with repetition, as if that's a magic formula. What's important is that we pray with a heart attitude that pleases God—with humility, sincerity, and faith.

Whether we're praying with others or on our own, our aim is to be fully present and genuine. We want to seek God earnestly, giving Him our full attention, and offer Him the "real" us. Of course there will be times we'll be tempted to pray only out of duty, but we must engage our hearts and minds, then fight off distractions.

One way to begin is by singing a hymn or reading Scripture; this brings our focus to God and His truth, and it stirs our affection and praise. It helps us to be still and know that He is God, draw near to Him with reverence, and develop that heart attitude we want to have—humility, sincerity, and faith.

We invite His Spirit to fill us, to lead our minds to truth and our hearts to worship. We listen to Him by receiving His Word, whether we're reading a Bible sitting in front of us or recalling a truth we've learned from it.

Then we respond to Him. We express awe at who He is and our desire to honor Him. We offer praise, thanks, and love. We confess wrongdoings and ask for His help in every way. We demonstrate our belief in Him as we rely on His grace and power and as we ultimately submit ourselves to Him and His will.

Our response can take different forms. We might sing, which can further soften or open our hearts. We might journal, which, as we slow down to write, can bring more self-awareness and intentionality in our words to God. We might even sit in silent adoration and peace. We can choose to meditate on Scripture or turn a Bible verse into a prayer (picking a command or truth and asking God to help us live it out). It's another way of asking that God's will be done in our hearts and in the world.

Scripture shows us how transparent and expressive we can be with God, our refuge. Hannah poured out her sorrow and heartache to God. At times David cried out to Him in fear and guilt; other times he burst out with shouts of joy and praise. Again, we're bringing the "real" us to God, which will deepen our relationship with Him.

As we lift up our hearts and lives to God, offering all we can and inviting Him to live and work in every part of us, we are truly worshiping with all we are. And we're making the most of every opportunity for Him to receive glory in our lives.

Four

Prayers for Everyday Life

Prayer is not an exercise; it is the life.
—OSWALD CHAMBERS

*S*cripture presents prayer as a way of life. Jesus modeled ongoing communion with and dependence on the Father, regularly withdrawing to quiet places to pray. He taught that we should be persistent in prayer: "Keep on asking. . . . Keep on seeking. . . . Keep on knocking" (Matthew 7:7 NLT). The early believers were "constantly united in prayer" (Acts 1:14 NLT). Paul instructed Christians to devote themselves to it—to "pray continually" (1 Thessalonians 5:17 NIV).

When we follow Jesus in prioritizing this all-important experience of connecting with the Father, it changes how we live outside those prayer sessions. As we move through our day, we'll be quicker to turn our hearts to Him.

"Take your everyday, ordinary life—your sleeping, eating, going-to-work, and walking-around life—and place it before God as an offering" (Romans 12:1 THE MESSAGE). This is our act of worship as well as a way for us to stay close to the One we belong to.

"Abide in Me, and I in you," Jesus said (John 15:4 NKJV). Other translations tell us to "Stay joined to me" (CEV), "remain in me" (NET), and "live in me" (THE MESSAGE).

We can walk through every kind of moment in our lives— mundane or significant, distressing or delightful—in relationship with God. When we do, we're opening up ourselves to Him and depending on Him. We're joining our whole life with His life. We're inviting His powerful presence to reign in our hearts and lives, to bring glory to Himself through us. And we'll become happier as we know Him and love Him more all the time.

As we adopt this lifestyle of prayer, our relationship with God will increasingly define who we are. We'll be living out our true identity and joyfully fulfilling the purposes we were created for.

The following collection of prayers is intended to lead you through your daily life with God. Adapt them to fit your situation— whether you're praying on your own or with others, whether you're praying for yourself or for others.

Lift up your heart to your Father, who has His arms open wide to you.

As a deer longs for
streams of water,
so I long for you, O God.

—PSALM 42:1 NLT

DRAWING NEAR

God Most High,
we come to You in awe and reverence,
amazed at the privilege of being with You.
May we honor You rightly.
How grateful we are to have access to You
through Jesus, our Great High Priest!
We come with confidence
in Your grace and goodness.
We humble ourselves before You
and bow in worship
before the One who is lifted up.

—C. M.

I am bending my knee
in the eye of the Father who created me,
in the eye of the Son who purchased me,
in the eye of the Spirit who cleansed me,
in friendship and affection.

—ANN MACDONALD (19TH C.)

In confidence of your goodness and great mercy,
O Lord,
I draw near to You,
as a sick person to the healer,
as one hungry and thirsty to the fountain of life,
a creature to the creator,
a desolate soul to my own tender comforter.
Behold, in You is everything I can or should desire.
You are my salvation and my redemption,
my hope and my strength.
Bring joy, therefore, to the soul of Your servant;
for to You, O Lord,
have I lifted my soul.

—THOMAS À KEMPIS (1380–1471)

Give us grace, almighty Father,
to address You with all our hearts
as well as with our lips.
You are everywhere present;
from You no secrets can be hidden.
Teach us to fix our thoughts on You,
reverently and with love.

—JANE AUSTEN (1775–1817)

Open wide the window of our spirits, O Lord,
and fill us full of light;
Open wide the door of our hearts,
that we may receive . . . You
with all our powers of adoration and love.
—CHRISTINA ROSSETTI (1830–1894)

O Lord, take away all coldness,
all wanderings of the thoughts,
and fix our souls on You and Your love,
O merciful Lord and Savior.
—EDWARD WHITE BENSON (1829–1896)

Eternal Light, shine into our hearts,
Eternal Goodness, deliver us from evil,
Eternal Power, be our support,
Eternal Wisdom, scatter the darkness of our ignorance,
Eternal Pity, have mercy upon us;
that with all our heart and mind and soul and strength
we may seek Your face
and be brought by Your infinite mercy
to Your holy presence.
—ST. ALCUIN OF YORK (C. 732–804)

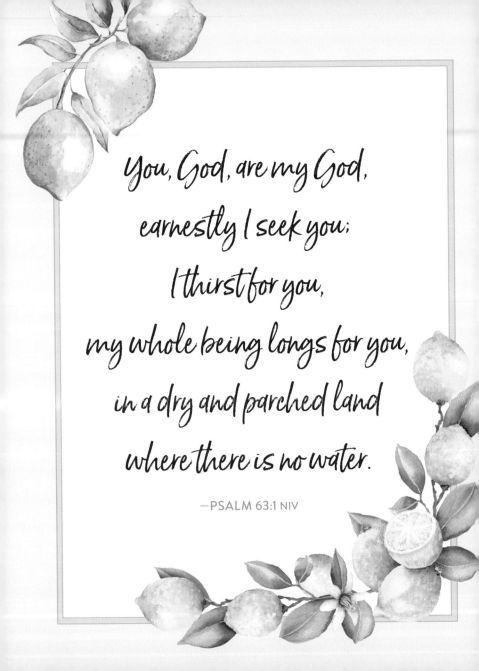

You, God, are my God,
earnestly I seek you;
I thirst for you,
my whole being longs for you,
in a dry and parched land
where there is no water.

—PSALM 63:1 NIV

LISTENING TO AND
WELCOMING HIS SPIRIT

God, You have removed the veil
so that nothing stands between us.
You are personally present—right here with me.
As I sit in Your presence now,
guard my heart and mind
as I give You my full attention.
I am still. I know that You are God.
I take time to ponder quietly that . . .

> You are the One who laid the earth's foundations,
> the One who gave me life,
> > the One reigning over all that exists throughout
> > > every age.

I honor You and exalt You, almighty God!
I listen for Your voice.
I meditate on Your Word.
I invite Your Spirit of Truth
to reveal more of Yourself to me
and lead me in Your ways.

—C. M.

Lord, You have given us Your Word
for a light to shine on our path.
Inspire us to meditate on that Word,
and follow its teaching,
that we may find in it the light
that shines more and more until it is perfect day.

—ST. JEROME (347–420)

Speak, Lord, for Your servant hears.
Grant us ears to hear,
eyes to see,
wills to obey,
hearts to love;
then declare what You will.

—CHRISTINA ROSSETTI (1830–1894)

Lord Jesus, open our ears,
heal our wounds,
and purify our lives,
as You did those who came to You.
Then we may hear and perceive what is true
amidst the sounds of the world
and find wholeness in ourselves.

—ORIGEN OF ALEXANDRIA (C. 185–254), ADAPTED

Lord, let not our souls be busy inns
that have no room for You,
but quiet homes of prayer and praise,
where You may find fit company,
where the needful cares of life
are wisely ordered and put away,
and wide, sweet spaces kept for You;
where holy thoughts pass up and down
and fervent longings watch and wait Your coming.
—JULIAN OF NORWICH (1342–C. 1416)

I need You to teach me day by day,
according to each day's opportunities and needs....
My ears are dull, so that I cannot hear Your voice.
My eyes are dim, so that I cannot see Your gifts.
You alone can quicken my hearing,
improve my sight,
and cleanse and renew my heart.
Teach me to sit at Your feet and to hear Your Word.
—ST. JOHN HENRY NEWMAN (1801–1890)

Lord, help me clear my mind to make room for You.
I'm ready to receive what You want to give.
—C. M.

Enlighten us, O God, by Your Spirit,
in the understanding of Your Word,
and grant us the grace to receive it
in true fear and humility,
that we may learn to put our trust in You,
to fear and honor You,
by glorifying Your Holy Name in all our life,
and to give You . . . love and obedience.
—JOHN CALVIN (1509–1564)

ADORING AND PRAISING GOD

Almighty God, whose glory the heavens are telling,
the earth His power,
and the seas His might,
and whose greatness all feeling and thinking creatures
everywhere proclaim;
to You belong glory, honor, might,
greatness, and magnificence
now and forever.
—LITURGY OF ST. JAMES

Our Father in heaven,
Reveal who you are.
Set the world right;
Do what's best—
as above, so below.
Keep us alive with three square meals.
Keep us forgiven with you
and forgiving others.
Keep us safe from ourselves and the Devil.
You're in charge!
You can do anything you want!
You're ablaze in beauty!

—MATTHEW 6:9–13 THE MESSAGE

You are holy, Lord, the only God,
and Your deeds are wonderful.
You are strong.
You are great.
You are the Most High.
You are Almighty.
You, Holy Father, are King of heaven and earth.
You are Three and One, Lord God, all Good.
You are Good, all Good, supreme Good,
Lord God, living and true.
You are love. You are wisdom.
You are humility. You are endurance.
You are rest. You are peace.
You are joy and gladness.
You are justice and moderation.
You are all our riches, and You suffice for us.
You are beauty.
You are gentleness.
You are our protector.
You are our guardian and defender.
You are our courage.
You are our haven and our hope.
You are our faith, our great consolation.
You are our eternal life, Great and Wonderful Lord,
God Almighty, Merciful Savior.

—ST. FRANCIS OF ASSISI (1181–1226)

Great, O Lord, is Your kingdom, Your power, and Your
    glory;
great also is Your wisdom, Your goodness, Your justice,
    Your mercy;
and for all these we bless You,
and will magnify Your name forever and ever.
    —GEORGE WITHER (1588–1667)

You move us to delight in praising You;
for You have made us for Yourself,
and our hearts are restless until they rest in You.
    —ST. AUGUSTINE OF HIPPO (354–430)

It is truly right and good,
always and everywhere,
with our whole heart and mind and voice,
to praise You,
the invisible, almighty, and eternal God,
and Your only begotten Son, Jesus Christ our Lord. . . .
How wonderful and beyond our knowing, O God,
is Your mercy and lovingkindness to us,
that to redeem a slave, You gave a Son.
    —BOOK OF COMMON PRAYER

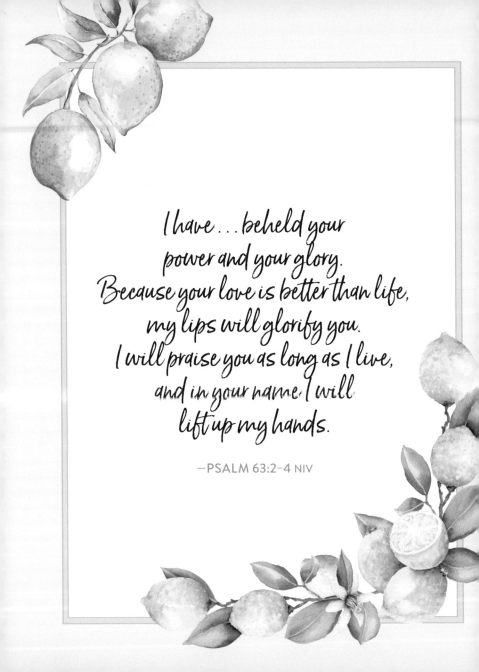

I have . . . beheld your
power and your glory.
Because your love is better than life,
my lips will glorify you.
I will praise you as long as I live,
and in your name I will
lift up my hands.

—PSALM 63:2–4 NIV

O Lord Jesus Christ, make me worthy to understand
the profound mystery of Your holy incarnation,
which You have worked for our sake and for our
    salvation.
Truly there is nothing so great and wonderful as this,
that You, my God, who are the Creator of all things,
should become a creature,
so that we should become like God.
You have humbled Yourself and made Yourself small
that we might be made mighty.
You have taken the form of a servant,
so that You might confer upon us a royal and divine
    beauty.
You, who are beyond our understanding,
have made Yourself understandable to us in Jesus
    Christ. . . .
You who are the untouchable One,
have made Yourself touchable to us. . . .
Blessed are You, O Lord, for coming to earth as a man.
You were born that You might die,
and in dying that You might save us.
O marvelous and indescribable love!

—ANGELA DA FOLIGNO (1248–1309)

Jesus, preaching good tidings to the poor,
proclaiming release to the captives,
setting at liberty those who are bound,
I adore You.
Jesus, friend of the poor,
feeder of the hungry,
healer of the sick,
I adore You.
Jesus, denouncing the oppressor,
instructing the simple,
going about doing good,
I adore You.
Jesus, teacher of patience,
pattern of gentleness,
prophet of the kingdom of heaven,
I adore You.

—*A BOOK OF PRAYERS FOR STUDENTS*

God, of Your goodness give me Yourself,
for You are enough for me.
And only in You do I have everything.

—JULIAN OF NORWICH (1342–C. 1416)

Praise to the Lord, the almighty, the King of creation!
O my soul, praise Him, for He is your health and
　　salvation!
Come, all who hear; brothers and sisters draw near,
praise Him in glad adoration!
Praise to the Lord, above all things so mightily reigning;
keeping us safe at His side and so gently sustaining.
Have you not seen all you have needed has been
met by His gracious ordaining?
Praise to the Lord, who when darkness and sin are
　　abounding,
who when the godless are rampant, all goodness
　　confounding,
shines with His light, scatters the terror of night,
safely His people surrounding.
Praise to the Lord, who shall prosper our work and
　　defend us;
surely His goodness and mercy shall daily attend us.
Ponder anew what the almighty can do,
who with His love will befriend us.
Praise to the Lord—O let all that is in me adore Him!
All that has life and breath, come now with praises
　　before Him!
Let the "Amen!" sound from His people again;
gladly with praise we adore Him!
　　—JOACHIM NEANDER (1650–1680)

CONFESSING

O Lord God, our Father most loving,
we would not, even if we could, conceal anything
      from You,
but rejoice rather that You know us as we are
and see every desire and every motive of our hearts.
Help us, Lord, to strip off every mask and every veil
when we come into Your presence,
and to spread before You every thought
and every secret of our being,
that they may be forgiven, purified, amended, and
      blessed by You;
through Jesus Christ our Lord.
      —CHARLES JOHN VAUGHAN (1816–1897)

Almighty God,
to whom all hearts are open, all desires known,
and from whom no secrets are hid,
cleanse the thoughts of my heart
by the inspiration of Your Holy Spirit,
that I may perfectly love You,
and worthily magnify Your holy name.
      —GREGORIAN SACRAMENTARY

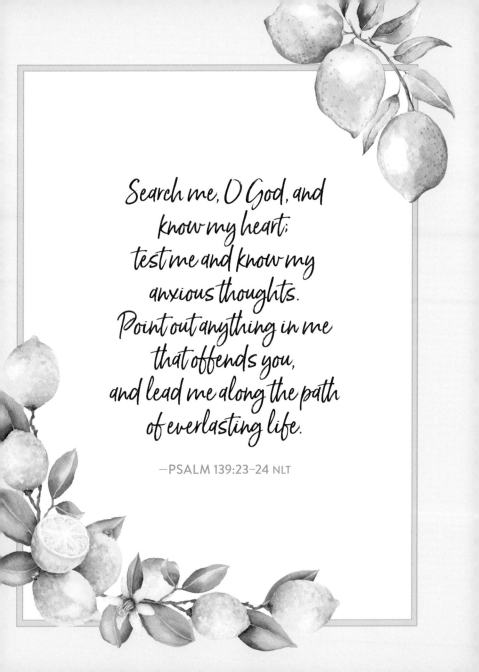

Search me, O God, and
know my heart;
test me and know my
anxious thoughts.
Point out anything in me
that offends you,
and lead me along the path
of everlasting life.

—PSALM 139:23–24 NLT

Spirit, help me receive the truth and light of the Word.
Help me see the sins I don't notice
and the ones I can't seem to escape.
Give me the strength to face my sins and deal with them.
Lead me in repentance.
Set me free and bring me closer to You.
Heal me, great God, and let me walk in the light
      with You.
I praise You for Your mercy and kindness to me.

—C. M.

Forgive me my sins, O Lord;
the sins of my present and the sins of my past,
the sins of my soul and the sins of my body,
the sins which I have done to please myself
and the sins which I have done to please others.
Forgive me my casual sins and my deliberate sins,
and those which I have labored so
to hide that I have hidden them even from myself.
Forgive me, O Lord, forgive all my sins,
for Jesus' sake.

—THOMAS WILSON (1663–1755)

GIVING THANKS

Lord of the universe, You are amazing!
You designed and formed the heavens and earth
and all they contain.
You open Your hand to provide
and satisfy the desires of every living thing.
From Your abundance You have poured out blessings
and piled them up.
You are worthy, great God, of all honor and praise!
Thank You for creating me,
for making me exactly the way I am and in Your image.
Thank You for giving me senses
to experience Your marvelous world,
for surrounding me with beauty
that captures my heart and fills me with wonder.
Thank You for giving me breath after breath
to experience You in myriad ways.
Truly, in You I live and move and have my being.
Lord, keep my soul awake to Your gifts I live with daily!
I exalt You and lift up to You a grateful heart.
I worship You for Your infinite power and love,
for Your endless generosity and kindness.

—C. M.

Now, our God, we give
you thanks, and praise
your glorious name.

—1 CHRONICLES 29:13 NIV

O God our Father, we thank You
for all the bright things of life.
Help us to see them,
and to count them,
and to remember them,
that our lives may flow in ceaseless praise;
for the sake of Jesus Christ our Lord.

—J. H. JOWETT (1846–1923)

Heavenly Father,
receive my evening sacrifice of praise. . . .
I thank You for all the known
and unknown mercies of another day,
for all the blessings of this life,
for all the means of grace,
for all the riches of Your salvation,
and for the hope of glory, that blessed hope,
the coming of our Lord Jesus Christ
and our gathering together unto Him.
We are one day nearer to that day.
Teach us to live every day
as those whose citizenship is in heaven.

—HANDLEY CARR GLYN MOULE (1841–1920)

For the beauty of the earth,
for the glory of the skies,
for the love which from our birth
over and around us lies.
For the wonder of each hour
of the day and of the night,
hill and vale and tree and flower,
sun and moon and stars of light.
For the joy of human love,
brother, sister, parent, child,
friends on earth, and friends above,
for all gentle thoughts and mild.
For Yourself, best gift divine,
to the world so freely given,
agent of God's grand design:
peace on earth and joy in heaven.
Christ, our Lord, to You we raise
this, our hymn of grateful praise.
—FOLLIOTT S. PIERPOINT (1835–1917)

May the Lord be blessed forever for the great gifts
He has continually heaped upon me,
and may all that He has created praise Him.
—ST. TERESA OF ÁVILA (1515–1582)

ASKING FOR HELP

God, You are the source of all that is worth having.
Every good gift in this world comes from You!
You are a generous Father,
providing what we need
and delighting in showering blessings on us.
As we think of You even giving up Your Son for us,
may we never assume You'd hold back Your generosity.
Jesus taught us to knock, ask, seek,
and persist!
So we ask You now to give us
what we need and hope for—
as it pleases You.
We worship the One on the throne
and open up our hands to receive from the Giver of life.
We say that You're good,
we need You,
and we're glad to rely on You.
Help us to honor You as we steward whatever You give,
hold loosely whatever we have,
and always love You, the Giver, more than the gifts.

—C. M.

O Lord, to be turned from You is to fall,
to turn to You is to rise,
and to stand in Your presence is to live forever.
Grant us in all our duties Your help,
in all our perplexities Your guidance,
in all our dangers Your protection,
and in all our sorrows Your peace.
—ST. AUGUSTINE OF HIPPO (354–430), ADAPTED

We ask not for wealth, reputation, honor, or prosperity;
we pray for a calm and peaceful spirit,
for every opportunity of leading a holy life,
and for circumstances that are most free from
      temptation.
We pray for Your preserving grace.
      —HENRY THORNTON (1760–1815)

Dear Lord Jesus, I shall have this day only once;
before it is gone,
help me to do all the good I can,
so that today is not a wasted day.
      —STEPHEN GRELLET (1773–1855)

Teach me, O Father, how to ask You silently
for Your help moment after moment. . . .
If I am uneasy or troubled, enable me,
by Your grace,
quickly to turn to You.
May nothing come between me and You today.
May I will, do, and say just what You,
my loving and tender Father,
would have me will, do, and say.

—EDWARD BOUVERIE PUSEY (1800–1882),
ADAPTED

O Lord, send down Your grace to help me,
that I may glorify Your name. . . .
Grant me humility, love, and obedience. . . .
Implant in me the root of all blessings:
the reverence of You in my heart.

—ST. JOHN CHRYSOSTOM (C. 347–407)

God, I need You every hour.
I ask You to meet my needs
as I offer up my hopes and dreams to You.

—C. M.

TRUSTING AND SUBMITTING

I pray to You, O Lord,
who are the supreme Truth,
and all truth is from You.
I pray to You, O Lord,
who are the highest Wisdom,
and all the wise depend on You for their wisdom.
You are the supreme Joy,
and all who are happy owe it to You.
You are the highest Good,
and all goodness comes from You.
You are the Light of minds,
and all receive their understanding from You.
I love You, , , ,
I seek You, follow You, and am prepared to serve You.
I desire to live under Your power,
for You are the King of all.
—KING ALFRED THE GREAT OF WESSEX (849–899)

Boundless is Your love for me,
Boundless then my trust will be.
—ROBERT BRIDGES (1844–1930)

O Lord, take full possession of my heart,
raise there Your throne,
and command there as You do in heaven.
Being created by You,
let me live for You;
being created for You,
let me always act for Your glory;
being redeemed by You,
let me give to You what is Yours;
and let my spirit cling to You alone,
for Your name's sake.

—JOHN WESLEY (1703–1791)

Dear Lord Jesus, I give You my hands to do Your work.
I give You my feet to go Your way.
I give You my eyes to see as You see.
I give You my tongue to speak Your words.
I give You my mind that You may think in me. . . .
Above all I give You my heart that You may love
        in me—
love God the Father and love all humankind.
I give You my whole self, Lord Jesus,
that You may grow in me,
so that it is You who lives in me.

—"THE GRAIL PRAYER," ANONYMOUS

Show me your ways, LORD. . . .
Guide me in your truth
and teach me,
for you are God my Savior,
and my hope is in
you all day long.

—PSALM 25:4–5 NIV

My heart I give You, Lord, eagerly and entirely.
—JOHN CALVIN (1509–1564)

Lord, I am Yours; I was born for You.
What is Your will for me?
—ST. TERESA OF ÁVILA (1515–1582)

O Lord, may I not desire health or life except to
spend them for You, with You, and in You.
You alone know what is good for me;
do, therefore, what seems best to You.
Give to me, or take from me.
Conform my will to Yours.
—BLAISE PASCAL (1623–1662)

You alone know best what is for my good.
As I am not my own but altogether Yours,
So neither do I desire that my will be done,
but Yours,
nor will I have any will but Yours.
—ST. FRANCIS BORGIA (1510–1572)

My Father, I abandon myself into Your hands.
Do with me as You will.
Whatever You may do with me,
I thank You.
I am prepared for anything.
I accept everything,
provided Your will is fulfilled in me and in all creatures.
I ask for nothing more, my God.
I place my soul in Your hands,
I give it to You, my God,
with all the love of my heart,
because I love You.
And for me it is a necessity of love,
this gift of myself,
this placing of myself in Your hands,
in boundless confidence,
because You are my Father.

—CHARLES DE FOUCAULD (1858–1916)

Lord, today I will trust You.
Instead of worrying, I submit my concerns to You
because You are the wise Almighty
and because You love me.

—C. M.

BUILDING INTIMACY WITH GOD

O my God Jesus, I am in every way unworthy of You.
Yet, like Joseph of Arimathea, I want to offer a space
    for You.
He offered His own tomb; I offer my heart.
Enter the darkness of my heart,
as Your body entered the darkness of Joseph's tomb.
And make me worthy to receive You,
driving out all sin that I may be filled with Your spiritual
    light.
    —ST. BONAVENTURE (C. 1217–1274)

Lord Jesus, stay with us, . . .
be our companion in our way,
kindle our hearts,
and awaken hope,
that we may know You as You are revealed in Scripture
and the breaking of bread.
Grant this for the sake of Your love.
    —BOOK OF COMMON PRAYER

O God,
be all my love, all my hope, all my striving.
Let my thoughts and words flow from You,
my daily life be in You,
and every breath I take be for You.

—ST. JOHN CASSIAN (C. 360–435)

We ask You, Lord, to purify our hearts
that they may be worthy to become Your dwelling place.
Let us never fail to find room for You.
Come and abide in us,
that we also may abide in You.

—WILLIAM TEMPLE, ARCHBISHOP OF
CANTERBURY (1881–1944)

Grant, O Lord, that we may cling to You without parting,
worship You without wearying,
serve You without wavering,
faithfully seek You,
happily find You,
and forever possess You,
the only God,
blessed now and forever.

—ST. ANSELM OF CANTERBURY (1033–1109)

O God, our true life,
to know You is life,
to serve You is freedom,
to enjoy You is a kingdom,
to praise You is the joy and happiness of the soul.
I praise and bless and adore You,
I worship You,
I glorify You.
I give thanks to You for Your great glory.
I humbly beg You to live with me,
to reign in me,
to make this heart of mine a holy temple,
a fit habitation for Your divine majesty.

—ST. AUGUSTINE OF HIPPO (354–430)

God be in my head, and in my understanding;
God be in my eyes, and in my looking;
God be in my mouth, and in my speaking;
God be in my heart, and in my thinking;
God be at my end, and at my departing.

—*SARUM PRIMER* (1558)

O good Jesus, my Master,
teach me.
O good Jesus, Prince of peace,
give me peace.
O good Jesus, my Refuge,
receive me.
O good Jesus, my Pastor,
feed my soul.
O good Jesus, Eternal Truth,
instruct me.
O good Jesus, life of the blessed,
make me live in You.
O good Jesus, Model of patience,
comfort me.
O good Jesus, meek and humble of heart,
make my heart like Yours.
O good Jesus, my Redeemer,
save me.
O good Jesus, my God and my all,
possess me.
O good Jesus, the true Way,
direct me.

—CATHOLIC PRAYER (1916)

GROWING AND TRANSFORMING

May Your Spirit take over me,
showing me Your beauty, truth, and light.
Fill me with Your peace, joy, and love.
Change me in Your presence, God.
Reshape me to be more like You.
Enter my life in new ways
and make it brighter and more beautiful to reflect You.
May my life bring You joy
and carry Your goodness to others.

—C. M.

Have Thine own way, Lord,
Have Thine own way;
Thou art the Potter,
I am the clay.
Mold me and make me,
After Thy will,
While I am waiting,
Yielded and still.

—ADELAIDE POLLARD (1862–1934)

You are gentle with us, like a mother with her children. . . .
Tenderly You draw us from hatred and judgment.
You comfort us in sorrow and bind up our wounds. . . .
Jesus, by Your dying we are born to new life;
by Your anguish and labor we come forth in joy.
Despair turns to hope through Your sweet goodness;
through Your gentleness we find comfort in fear.
Your warmth gives life to the dead.
Your touch makes sinners righteous.
Lord Jesus, in Your mercy, heal us;
in Your love and tenderness, remake us;
in Your compassion, bring grace and forgiveness.
May Your love prepare us for the beauty of heaven.

—ST. ANSELM OF CANTERBURY (1033–1109)

Lord, what we know not, teach us.
Lord, what we have not, give us.
Lord, what we are not, make us.

—ST. AUGUSTINE OF HIPPO (354–430)

God, right now I see that I need to grow in certain areas.
I'm willing to take a step toward transformation today.
Do a mighty work in me and make me more like You.

—C. M.

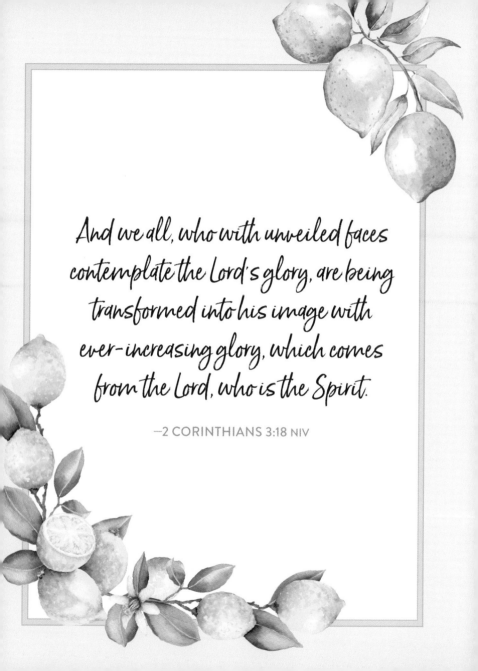

And we all, who with unveiled faces contemplate the Lord's glory, are being transformed into his image with ever-increasing glory, which comes from the Lord, who is the Spirit.

—2 CORINTHIANS 3:18 NIV

O Lord God, root out and destroy
whatever the adversary has planted in me.
Grow my understanding
and continue Your good work in me,
so I may serve You, obey You, and see You.
Give me love, chastity, and faith.
Give me all things You know will benefit my soul.
O Lord, work good in me
and provide me with what You know I need.

—ST. COLUMBANUS (C. 543–615), ADAPTED

Grant me the grace, O Lord,
to know what is worth knowing,
love what is worth loving,
praise what delights You most,
value what is precious to You,
and reject what is evil in Your eyes.
Give us discernment,
to judge between things that appear similar,
and to search out and do
those things that delight You.

—THOMAS À KEMPIS (1380–1471), ADAPTED

Our Father, You called us and saved us
in order to make us like Your Son,
our Lord Jesus Christ.
Day by day, change us by the work of Your Holy Spirit
so that we may grow more like Him
in all that we think and say and do,
to His glory.

—SØREN KIERKEGAARD (1813–1855)

O Love, O God, You created me;
in Your love recreate me.
O Love, You redeemed me;
fill up and redeem for Yourself in me
whatever part of Your love has fallen into neglect within me.
O Love, O God, You made me Yours,
in the blood of Christ purchased me;
in Your truth sanctify me.
O Love, You chose me as Yours;
grant that I may cling to You with my whole being.
O Love, O God, You loved me first;
grant that with my whole heart,
and with my whole soul,
and with my whole strength,
I may love You.

—ST. GERTRUDE THE GREAT (1256–1302)

WORSHIPING THROUGH ORDINARY TASKS

Lord, You have given us so much.
As You reach down
and meet with us through Your Spirit,
heaven touches earth,
and You make our lives sacred;
You make the ordinary holy.
Give me grace to remember this
each hour of the day.
May I greet my everyday tasks with gratitude,
seeing them as practices to treat with honor,
as ways I can experience You more deeply.
May I see my everyday moments as opportunities to worship,
to depend on You and abide with You,
and to do all things with joy and love for You in my heart.
Lord, help me to use Your great gift of life faithfully.

—C. M.

O Father, light up the small duties of this day;
may they shine with the beauty of Your face.
May I believe that glory can dwell
in the commonest task every day.

—ST. AUGUSTINE OF HIPPO (354–430)

Lord, may I be wakeful at sunrise to begin a new day for You;
cheerful at sunset for having done my work for You;
thankful at moonrise and under starshine for the beauty of
  the universe.
And may I add what little may be in me to Your great world.
  —THE ABBOT OF GREVE (12TH C.)

Lord, in union with Your love,
unite my work with Your great work, and perfect it.
As a drop of water poured into a river
is taken up into the activities of the river,
so may my labor become part of Your work.
Thus may those among whom I live and work
be drawn into Your love.
  —ST. GERTRUDE THE GREAT (1256–1302)

Into Your hands, O Lord, I commend myself this day.
Let Your presence be with me to its close.
Strengthen me to remember that,
in whatever good work I do, I am serving You.
Give me a diligent and watchful spirit,
that I may seek in all things to know Your will,
and knowing it, gladly to perform it,
to the honor or Your name.
  —GELASIAN SACRAMENTARY (8TH C.)

O Lord, give Your blessing, I pray, to my daily work,
that I may do it in faith and heartily,
as to the Lord and not to men.
All my powers of body and mind are Yours,
and I devote them to Your service.
Sanctify them, and the work in which I am engaged,
and bless my efforts
so they may bring forth in me the fruits of true wisdom.
—THOMAS ARNOLD (1795–1842)

Lord, be with me, and help me by Your Spirit,
to perform all my duties to Your praise.
—ELIZABETH FRY (1780–1845)

Almighty God,
in whose hands are all our human powers,
grant that we may not waste the life
You have given us on useless trifles.
Enable us by Your Holy Spirit to shun sloth and negligence,
so that every day we may perform the tasks You have given us,
and have, in everything we do,
such success as will give most glory to You;
for the sake of Jesus Christ.
—SAMUEL JOHNSON (1709–1784)

Jesus, You washed the feet of Your disciples,
taking on an ordinary, mundane task,
even one meant for a servant.
In Your life of worship,
You spent Yourself for others and for the Father.
May I do the same, serving with eagerness and joy,
privileged to follow in Your footsteps
and fulfilled by living out my purpose.
May my work be an offering, not a burden,
and may it truly help and bless another.

—C. M.

Almighty God our heavenly Father,
You declare Your glory and show forth Your handiwork
in the heavens and in the earth:
Deliver us in our various occupations from the
        service of self alone,
that we may do the work You give us to do
in truth and beauty and for the common good;
for the sake of Him who came among us as one who
        serves,
Your Son Jesus Christ our Lord.

—BOOK OF COMMON PRAYER

Teach me, gracious Lord,
to begin my deeds with reverence,
to go on with obedience,
and to finish them in love;
and then to wait patiently in hope
and with cheerful confidence to look up to You,
whose promises are faithful and rewards infinite.

—GEORGE HICKES (1642–1715)

God, help me see today's ordinary tasks as ways I can
lovingly serve You.
Help me do them for Your sake and with a heart of praise.
Help me to remember You are with me in all things.

—C. M.

BEING OF SERVICE

God of love, help us to remember
that Christ has no body now on earth but ours,
no hands but ours,
no feet but ours.
Ours are the eyes to see the needs of the world.
Ours are the hands with which to bless everyone now.
Ours are the feet with which He is to go about doing good.

—ST. TERESA OF ÁVILA (1515–1582)

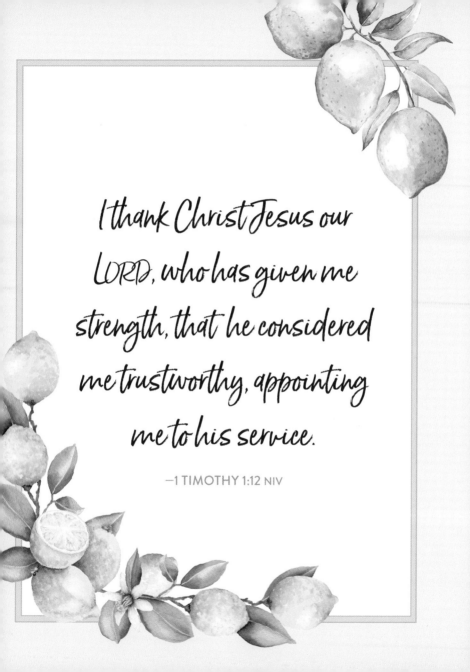

I thank Christ Jesus our LORD, who has given me strength, that he considered me trustworthy, appointing me to his service.

—1 TIMOTHY 1:12 NIV

Make us worthy, Lord,
to serve others throughout the world
who live and die in poverty or hunger.
Give them, through our hands,
this day their daily bread,
and give them, through our understanding love,
peace and joy.
—ST. TERESA OF CALCUTTA (1910–1997), ADAPTED

Lord, make me an instrument of Your peace:
where there is hatred, let me sow love;
where there is injury, pardon;
where there is doubt, faith;
where there is despair, hope;
where there is darkness, light;
where there is sadness, joy.
O divine Master, grant that I may not so much seek
to be consoled as to console,
to be understood as to understand,
to be loved as to love.
For it is in giving that we receive,
it is in pardoning that we are pardoned,
and it is in dying that we are born to eternal life.
—ST. FRANCIS OF ASSISI (1181–1226)

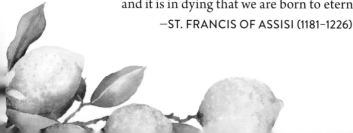

Use me, my Savior,
for whatever purpose you require
in whatever way you choose.
Here is my poor heart, an empty vessel;
fill it with your grace.
Here is my sinful, troubled soul;
refresh it with your love.
Take my heart for your home,
take my mouth to spread abroad your glory,
take my love for the advancement of believers.
—DWIGHT MOODY (1837–1899), ADAPTED

EXPRESSING JOY

As the hand is made for holding
and the eye for seeing,
You have created me for joy, O God.
Share with me in finding that joy everywhere:
in the violet's beauty,
in the lark's melody,
in the child's face,
in a mother's love,
in the purity of Jesus.
—TRADITIONAL SCOTTISH GAELIC PRAYER

Your Spirit, Lord, is around me
in the air I breathe.
Your glory, Lord, touches me
in the light that I see
and the fruitfulness of the earth
and the joys of its creatures.

—JOHN RUSKIN (1819–1900)

We give You thanks, most gracious God,
for the beauty of earth and sky and sea;
for the richness of mountains, plains, and rivers;
for the songs of birds and the loveliness of flowers.
We praise You for these good gifts. . . .
Grant that we may continue to grow
in our grateful enjoyment of Your abundant creation,
to the honor and glory of Your name,
now and forever.

—BOOK OF COMMON PRAYER

God, You thrill my heart with . . .
>   glowing sunrises in the vast sky,
>   bursts of flavor on my tongue,
>   adventures and discoveries in this wide world,
>   embraces from family,
>   laughter with friends.
You make me feel more alive through . . .
>   music that lifts my spirit,
>   exercise that invigorates my body,
>   challenges that stimulate my mind,
>   relationships that warm my heart,
>   worship that unites my soul with You.
You fill me with peace and joy when I realize . . .
>   that no danger, difficulty, or evil can overcome You;
>   Your light conquers darkness;
>   that nothing scares or surprises You;
>   Your awesome might and sovereignty reign;
>   that there is nothing You can't heal, renew, or remake;
>   Your creating, life-giving power has no limits;
>   that I belong to You, and I can take refuge in You,
>   that You created me out of Your joy, intending for me
>   to share in it,
>   that my life is about loving You,
>   and my name is written in heaven.

—C. M.

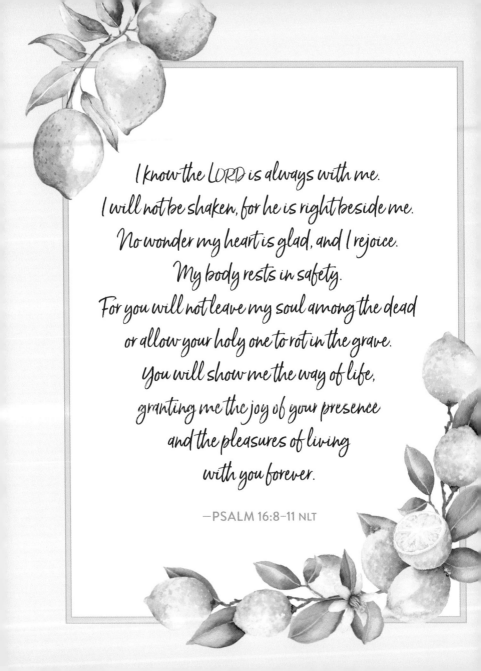

I know the LORD is always with me.
I will not be shaken, for he is right beside me.
No wonder my heart is glad, and I rejoice.
My body rests in safety.
For you will not leave my soul among the dead
or allow your holy one to rot in the grave.
You will show me the way of life,
granting me the joy of your presence
and the pleasures of living
with you forever.

—PSALM 16:8–11 NLT

Jesus, how sweet is the very thought of You!
You fill my heart with joy.
The sweetness of your love
surpasses the sweetness of honey. . . .
No words can express the joy of Your love. . . .
In Your love You listen to all my prayers,
even when my wishes are childish,
my words confused,
and my thoughts foolish.
And You answer my prayers,
not according to my own misdirected desires,
which would bring only bitter misery,
but according to my real needs,
which brings me sweet joy.
Thank You, Jesus, for giving Yourself to me.
   —ST. BERNARD OF CLAIRVAUX (1090–1153)

God, I join the psalmist in reveling in
Your stunning power,
heart-stopping beauty,
and absolute goodness!
Open my eyes to see You in action
and fill my heart with joyful celebration over Your
      wonders!
                              —C. M.

Five

Prayers for When You Need . . .

Prayer wonderfully clears the vision; steadies
the nerves; defines duty; stiffens the purpose;
sweetens and strengthens the spirit.

—S. D. GORDON

God gives us what we need for life—specifically to do life
His way.

We receive His power for daily challenges and godly living by
coming to know Him intimately (2 Peter 1:3) and by turning to
Him with our particular needs and requests.

Jesus taught His disciples to ask God for what they needed and
to remember that He is a good, generous Father. He said, "If your
children ask for a fish, do you give them a snake instead? Or if they

ask for an egg, do you give them a scorpion? Of course not! So if you sinful people know how to give good gifts to your children, how much more will your heavenly Father give the Holy Spirit to those who ask him" (Luke 11:11–13 NLT).

We run to the One who spreads His arms open wide to us, who never tires of us or turns us away. We find what we need in His presence—and only in His presence—with the One we belong to, the One we were made for.

In prayer, we rehearse our dependence on the Father and remember we are in His care. We come to Him lacking, and He stands ready to enable, empower, and provide in every area in which we are needy. His resources are always abundant and available.

We the vulnerable creatures, the limited, come to the Almighty, the limitless.

We come to the Healer, the Counselor, the Comforter, the Forgiver, the Protector, the Virtue Builder, the Strong Tower and Refuge.

Use these prayers for yourself, for someone else, for a group—substitute suitable pronouns to make them fit your situation. They are simply inspirations for prayer that can lead you into the assurance of the Father's love and provision, calming and strengthening the soul.

ASSURANCE OF FORGIVENESS

Lord, just as Your love and mercy prompted You
to come down from Your high throne
to rescue us,
so Your love and mercy reach out
to my repentant heart now.
Jesus, on earth You said, "I came to save the world,
to give you life,
to make you right with the Father
and bring you back to Him."
You locked eyes with people and powerfully proclaimed,
"Your sins are forgiven."
Help me sense that You do the same with me now.

Jesus, I imagine You being my advocate with the Father.
I imagine Your hand of blessing upon me.
Spirit of God, give me faith to receive this gift of grace.
Help me believe You and remember You never lie.
If You say it . . . it's true!
I'm forgiven and free
and can abide with You in peace and joy!

—C. M.

O eternal Mercy, You cover Your creatures' faults! . . .
You say to those who leave deadly sin behind
and return to You:
"I will not remember that you had ever offended me."
O unspeakable mercy! . . .
You say of those who persecute You:
"I want you to pray for them
so that I can be merciful to them." . . .
Your mercy is life-giving.
It is the light in which both the upright and sinners
discover Your goodness. . . .
In mercy You cleansed us in the blood;
in mercy You kept company with Your creatures.
       —ST. CATHERINE OF SIENA (1347–1380)

O God, we belong to You utterly.
You are such a Father
that You take our sins from us
and throw them behind Your back.
You clean our souls
as Your Son also washed the disciples' feet.
We hold up our hearts to You:
make them what they must be.
       —GEORGE MACDONALD (1824–1905)

Lord, I praise You that
forgiveness is Your will for me.
You set out to rescue me
from the kingdom of darkness
and bring me into Your kingdom of light.
You did not want me doomed to stay stuck in my sin
and be destroyed by it.
You conquered my sin and
reconciled me to Yourself,
bringing me close to Your heart,
assuring me of Your eternal love!
I praise You that
sharing in Your divine life
is Your will for me.
In Your presence I am able to
marvel at Your glory,
be healed,
be restored and transformed to be like Jesus,
become holy to serve You,
be raised to new life,
know infinite joy in Your kingdom.
I praise You that
Your will is so good and perfect,
and that You accomplish it!

—C. M.

COMFORT

Comfort . . . all who are cast down and faint of heart
amidst the sorrows and difficulties of the world;
and grant that,
by the quickening power of the Holy Spirit,
they may be lifted up to You with hope and courage,
and enabled to go upon their way
rejoicing in Your love.
　　—RICHARD MEUX BENSON (1824–1915)

I praise You that
You are the God of all comfort.
You refresh the weary,
replenish the weak,
and revive the faint.
You bring joy to those with sorrow
and peace to those who mourn.
Now as our burdens are heavy,
and we are tired and discouraged,
we turn to You,
grateful that we can rest in You
and be restored by You.
　　—C. M.

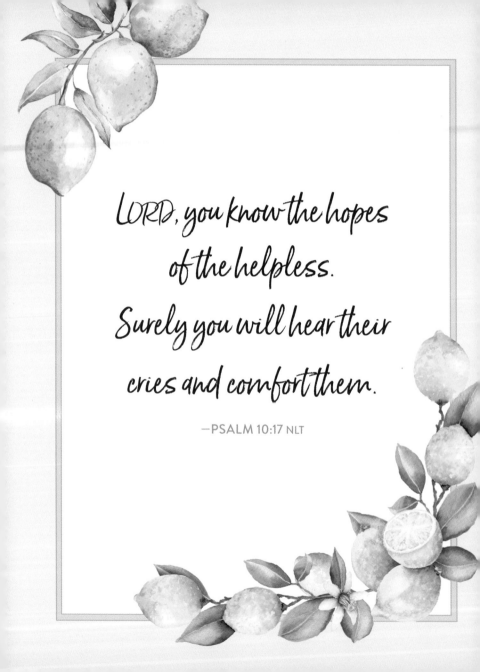

LORD, you know the hopes
of the helpless.
Surely you will hear their
cries and comfort them.

—PSALM 10:17 NLT

Write Your blessed name, O Lord, on my heart,
there to remain so indelibly engraved,
that no prosperity or adversity
will ever move me from Your love.
Be to me a strong tower of defense,
a comforter in tribulation,
a deliverer in distress,
a very present help in trouble,
and a guide to heaven
through the many temptations and dangers of this life.

—THOMAS À KEMPIS (1380–1471)

The day is Yours, O God, and the night also.
In the morning, You renew my strength;
in the evening, I find the shelter of Your wing.
You are my Sun,
and apart from You my toil is weary and blind,
and there is no glory in my joy.
You are my Shade,
for in You my restless soul finds rest.
Abiding God, enter fully into my life.

—JAMES MARTINEAU (1805–1900)

Although . . . You could rightly and properly
be a severe judge over us sinners . . .
now through Your mercy
implant in our hearts a comforting trust in Your
     fatherly love,
and let us experience the sweet and pleasant savor
of a childlike certainty
that we may joyfully call You Father,
knowing and loving You and calling on You in every
     trouble.

     —MARTIN LUTHER (1483–1546)

Almighty and eternal God,
You rule over all the affairs of the world.
There is not one circumstance so great
it cannot be subject to Your power,
nor so small to be under Your care.

     —QUEEN ANNE OF GREAT BRITAIN AND
       IRELAND (1665–1714), ADAPTED

Overcome my heartache
with Your healing comfort
and fill me with peace and hope.

     —C. M.

CONFIDENCE AND COURAGE

Father, hear the prayer we offer:
not for ease that prayer shall be,
but for strength, that we may ever
live our lives courageously.
  —LOVE MARIA WHITCOMB WILLIS (1824–1908)

O God, from everlasting to everlasting,
without beginning or ending of days,
replenish me with heavenly grace at the beginning of
    this day,
that I may be enabled to accept all its duties,
to perform all its labors,
to welcome all its mercies,
to meet all its trials,
and to advance through all it holds in store for me
with cheerful courage and a steady mind.
    —BOOK OF COMMON PRAYER

Lord, I do not ask for tasks equal to my strength;
I ask for strength equal to my tasks.
    —PHILLIPS BROOKS (1835–1893)

Lord, make possible for me by grace
what is impossible to me by nature.

—THOMAS À KEMPIS (1380–1471)

O King of glory and Lord of valors . . .
who has said, "Be of good cheer;
I have overcome the world":
be victorious in me Your servant.
Grant Your compassion to go before me,
Your compassion to come behind me.

—ST. ALCUIN OF YORK (C. 732–804)

Lord I hear you say,
"Be strong and courageous.
Do not be afraid;
do not be discouraged,
for the LORD your God will be with you
wherever you go" (Joshua 1:9 NIV).
Give me great faith in Your mighty power and
        perfect will.
Make me confident in how You have made me,
what You can do through me,
and what You want to accomplish.
Embolden me as I move forward in Your strength.

—C. M.

For you have been my
hope, Sovereign LORD, my
confidence since my youth.

—PSALM 71:5 NIV

Today I bind myself to the power of God
to hold and lead me;
His eye to watch,
His might to stay,
His ear to hearken to my need,
His wisdom to teach,
His hand to guide,
His shield to ward,
His Word to give me speech,
His heavenly host to be my guard.
—ST. PATRICK OF IRELAND (C. 387–C. 460)

Give us victory over the world and over ourselves. . . .
Make us valiant in all temptation and . . .
more than conquerors through Him who loved us.
—HENRY WARD BEECHER (1813–1887)

Father in heaven,
I call upon You and Your mighty power.
Fill me with Your strength,
and give me holy courage
as I do my work for You and Your kingdom.
—C. M.

Give me, O Lord, a steadfast heart,
which no unworthy thought can drag downward;
an unconquered heart,
which no tribulation can wear out;
an upright heart,
which no unworthy purpose may tempt aside.

—ST. THOMAS AQUINAS (1225–1274)

Lord, help me believe I can do hard things through You
because You strengthen me.
Fill me with Your Spirit
and write Your Word on my heart;
may Your truth give me courage
as I rely on Your power.
Give me perseverance and help me trust that,
even as I try and fail and try again,
You are changing me,
making me braver and more capable.
Shape me to be more like You
as I continue in the struggle.
Make me mature, strong, and confident
so I can do more for You and in You, my Lord.

—C. M.

What is before us, we know not, . . .
but this we know: . . . everything is ordered
with unerring wisdom and unbounded love
by You, our God, who is love.

—CHARLES SIMEON (1759–1836)

O Lord God, grant us always, whatever the world
    may say,
to content ourselves with what You say
and to care only for Your approval,
which will outweigh all worlds.

—CHARLES GEORGE GORDON (1833–1885)

Take from us, O God, all pride and vanity,
all boasting and self-assertion,
and give us the true courage that shows itself in
    gentleness,
the true wisdom that shows itself in simplicity,
and the true power that shows itself in modesty.

—CHARLES KINGSLEY (1819–1875)

Father, give me confidence and courage
make me bold in my faith for You.

—C. M.

GUIDANCE

God, I want Your guidance and direction in all I do.
Let Your wisdom counsel me,
Your hand lead me,
and Your arm support me.
I put myself into Your hands.
Breathe into my soul holy and heavenly desires.
Conform me to Your own image.
Make me like my Savior.
Enable me in some measure to live here on earth as He
      lived,
and to act in all things as He would have acted.

—ASHTON OXENDEN (1808–1892)

O Lord, take my mind and think through it;
take my lips and speak through them;
take my life and live out Your life;
take my heart and set it on fire with love for You;
and guide me ever by Your Holy Spirit.

—WILLIAM H. M. H. AITKEN (1841–1927)

O God, the King eternal,
whose light divides the day from the night
and turns the shadow of death into the morning:
Drive far from us all wrong desires,
incline our hearts to keep Your law,
and guide our feet into the way of peace;
that, having done Your will with cheerfulness
during the day, we may, when night comes,
rejoice to give You thanks; through Jesus Christ
    our Lord.
—WILLIAM REED HUNTINGTON (1838–1909)

O Lord, direct me in what to do
and what to leave undone.
—ELIZABETH FRY (1780–1845)

Lord God, almighty and everlasting Father,
You have brought me in safety to this new day:
preserve me with Your mighty power,
that I may not fall into sin, nor be overcome by adversity.
In all I do, direct me in fulfilling Your purpose.
—BOOK OF COMMON PRAYER

Steer the vessel of our life towards Yourself,
the tranquil haven of all storm-tossed souls.
Show us the course wherein we should go.
Renew a willing spirit within us.
Let Your Spirit curb our wayward senses,
and guide and enable us unto that which is our
       true good,
to keep Your laws,
and in all our works evermore
to rejoice in Your glorious and gladdening presence.
    —ST. BASIL OF CAESAREA (C. 329–379)

Guide us, teach us, and strengthen us, O Lord,
until we become what You would have us be:
pure, gentle, truthful, high-minded, courteous,
generous, able, dutiful, and useful,
for Your honor and glory.
      —CHARLES KINGSLEY (1819–1875)

Lord, fill me with Your Spirit of wisdom
so I may know what You want me to do.
Make it abundantly clear to me
what You want and what is best.
      —C. M.

HELP TO OBEY

God of love, bring me back to You.
Send Your Spirit to make me strong in faith
and active in good works. . . .
Father of love, source of all blessings,
help me to pass from my old life of sin
to the new life of grace.
Prepare me for the glory of Your kingdom.

—CATHOLIC PRAYER

Almighty and merciful God,
help us to deeply desire, wisely search out, and fulfill
all that is well pleasing to You today.
Reorder our worldly condition to the glory of
     Your Name.
Give us the knowledge, the desire, and the ability
to do all You require us to do.
May our path to You be safe, straightforward, and
     perfect to the end.

—ST. THOMAS AQUINAS (1225–1274), ADAPTED

Again he prayed,
"My Father, if there is no
other way than this,
drinking this cup to the dregs,
I'm ready.
Do it your way."

—MATTHEW 26:42 THE MESSAGE

O Lord our God, grant us grace
to desire You with a whole heart,
so that desiring You we may seek and find You;
and so finding You, may love You;
and loving You, may hate those sins which separate us
    from You,
for the sake of Jesus Christ.
  —ST. ANSELM OF CANTERBURY (1033–1109)

Father, set me free in the glory of Your will,
so that I will only as You will.
Your will be at once your perception and mine.
You alone are deliverance.
  —GEORGE MACDONALD (1824–1905)

O ever-living God,
may we have the mind of Christ.
Just as He stooped from heaven to the death of the cross,
may we humble ourselves,
believing, obeying, living, and dying to the glory of the
    Father,
for the same Jesus Christ's sake.
  —CHRISTINA ROSSETTI (1830–1894), ADAPTED

O Lord, prepare me for the events of the day;
for I know not what a day may bring forth.
Give me grace to deny myself;
to take up my cross
and to follow in the steps of my Lord and Master.
—MATTHEW HENRY (1662–1714)

O Lord our God,
in Your great goodness
and in the richness of Your mercy
You have protected me. . . .
With Your gift of true light,
pour into my heart the treasure of knowing You,
which enables me to do Your will.
—EASTERN ORTHODOX LITURGY

Give us, O Lord, a mind after Your own heart,
that we may delight to do Your will, O our God;
and let Your love be written on our hearts.
Give us courage and resolution to do our duty,
and a heart to be spent in Your service,
and in doing all the good that possibly we can
the few remaining days of our pilgrimage here on earth.
—JOHN TILLOTSON (1630–1694)

HOPE

O Christ, our Morning Star,
Splendor of Light Eternal,
shining with the glory of the rainbow,
come and waken us from the greyness of our apathy
and renew in us Your gift of hope.
        —ST. BEDE THE VENERABLE (672–735)

O Lord, the help of the helpless,
the hope of the hopeless,
the savior of the storm-tossed,
the harbor of voyagers,
the physician of the sick;
we pray to You.
O Lord, You know each of us and our petitions;
You know each house and its needs;
receive us all into Your kingdom;
make us children of light,
and bestow Your peace and love upon us.
        —ST. BASIL OF CAESAREA (C. 329–379)

Lord, I put my hope in You
because You are who You say You are.
You are the Light of the World,
the resurrection and the life, the great I AM.
No one created You; You are the One who is,
who always was, and who is still to come.
From beginning to end, You are God.
You are the epitome of goodness,
the source of life and blessing,
and we belong to You.
You are the supreme ruler of the universe;
You will ultimately crush the enemy
and defeat every evil.
You are able to do all things,
including protecting us, providing for us,
keeping us from stumbling, and guiding us.
You have promised to save us,
remake us, and bring us home to You—
and You always keep Your word.
So help me keep a firm grip on Your truth
and persist in hoping in You.
Make my belief strong
and my heart confident
because of who You are!

—C. M.

Give me, good Lord, a full faith,
a firm hope,
and a fervent charity,
a love for You incomparably above
the love of myself.

—ST. THOMAS MORE (1478–1535)

My God, I believe most firmly
that You watch over all who hope in You,
and that we can want for nothing
when we rely upon You in all things.
Therefore I am resolved for the future . . .
to cast all my cares upon You. . . .
Let others seek happiness
in their wealth and in their talents. . . .
As for me, my rock and my refuge,
my confidence in You fills me with hope.
For You, my divine protector,
alone have settled me in hope.
"This confidence can never be in vain.
No one, who has hoped in God,
has ever been confounded." . . .
All my hope is in You.

—BLESSED CLAUDE DE LA COLOMBIÈRE (1641–1682)

My hope is built on nothing less
Than Jesus' blood and righteousness
I dare not trust the sweetest frame
But wholly lean on Jesus' name
When darkness hides His lovely face
I rest on His unchanging grace
In every high and stormy gale
My anchor holds within the veil
His oath, His covenant, His blood
Support me in the whelming flood
When all around my soul gives way
He then is all my hope and stay
When He shall come with trumpet sound
Oh may I then in Him be found
Dressed in His righteousness alone
Faultless to stand before the throne
On Christ the solid Rock I stand
All other ground is sinking sand
All other ground is sinking sand
   —EDWARD MOTE (1797–1874)

O heart of Jesus,
treasure of tenderness,
You Yourself are my happiness,
my only hope.
   —ST. THÉRÈSE OF LISIEUX (1873–1897)

"Oh, that I might have my request, That God would grant what I hope for."

—JOB 6:8 NLT

JUSTICE

Lord, You know the pain I've endured
at the hands of others.
I give myself to You, the Healer.
I also submit to Your command
to love everyone around me,
including my enemies.
May I not repay evil for evil.
May my heart not wish harm
for those who have hurt me.
Instead, I pray for Your blessing on them.
Make me generous in grace and compassion,
and strong enough to live at peace with everyone.
I praise You because justice is in Your nature,
and I trust You to carry out justice as You see fit,
when You see fit.
You are God, and I am not.
You are on the throne, and You say,
"It is mine to avenge; I will repay" (Romans 12:19 NIV).
I give You honor, God,
and leave room for You to do
what Your wisdom says is just and right.

—C. M.

God, You've shown us what is good:
to act justly and to do what is fair to others.
You've sent Your Son to provide peace
and the bond of true fellowship.
Open our eyes to the needs of others—
of all the different types of people in this world.
Lead us out of our comfort zones
so we can bless and build bonds
with people who are different from us.
Lead us in respectful service toward one another,
treating each other as brothers and sisters.
May we be instruments in Your hands
as You bring Your kingdom of justice and peace.
May we spread Your goodness
and bring many to join us
in living close to You in Your glory and love.

C. M.

O God, the King of righteousness,
lead us in the ways of justice and peace,
inspire us to break down all tyranny and oppression,
to gain for every person what is due to them.
May each live for all and all care for each.

—WILLIAM TEMPLE (1881–1944), ADAPTED

Grant, O God, Your protection;
and in Your protection, strength;
and in strength, understanding;
and in understanding, knowledge;
and in knowledge, the knowledge of justice;
and in the knowledge of justice, the love of it;
and in the love, the love of existence;
and in the love of all existence, the love of God and all
    goodness.
        —ANCIENT WELSH PRAYER

God of love,
You see all the suffering, injustice, and misery in this
    world.
Have pity on what You have created.
In Your mercy look upon the poor,
the oppressed, the destitute,
and all who are heavy-laden.
Fill our hearts with deep compassion
for those who suffer,
and hasten the coming of
Your kingdom of justice and truth.
        —EUGÈNE BERSIER (1831–1889)

LOVE

O my God, let me walk in the way of love
which never seeks self in anything whatsoever.
But what love must it be?
It must be an ardent love,
a pure love,
a courageous love,
a love of charity,
a humble love,
and a constant love.
O Lord, give this love into my soul.

—DAME GERTRUDE MORE (1606-1633)

God, empower me to grasp Your tremendous love,
with its wild, astronomical dimensions,
reaching to the sky and beyond.
As I explore its breadth and experience its depths,
fill and expand my heart with it.
Make me rooted and established in it;
mature me in it.
And lead me in living in Your abundant life,
in the fullness of Your life and power.

—C. M.

Lord, give us hearts never to forget Your love;
but to remain there whatever we do. . . .
Let its flame never be quenched in our hearts;
let it grow and brighten,
till our whole souls are glowing and shining
with its light and warmth.

—JOHANN ARNDT (1555–1621)

Let the river of Your love run through my soul.
May my soul be carried by the current of Your love,
toward the wide, infinite ocean of heaven.
Stretch out my heart with Your strength,
as You stretch out the sky above the earth.
Smooth out any wrinkles of hatred or resentment.
Enlarge my soul that it may know more fully Your truth.

—GILBERT OF HOYLAND (D. 1172)

Good Jesus, my God and my all . . .
take from me all that displeases You
or hinders Your love in me.
Melt me with Your love, that I may be all love,
and with my whole being love You.
Good Jesus, You gave Yourself for me.
Give me of the fullness of Your love . . . that I may love You.

—EDWARD BOUVERIE PUSEY (1800–1882)

I call on you, my God, for
you will answer me;
turn your ear to me and hear my prayer.
Show me the wonders of your great love,
you who save by your right hand
those who take refuge in
you from their foes
Keep me as the apple of your eye;
hide me in the shadow of your wings

—PSALM 17:6–8 NIV

Love is who You are.
Loved is what I am.
You see my faults and weaknesses,
but embrace me anyway.
You choose tenderness and grace.
You make me beautiful in Your love.
You say I am Your beloved—
and, Lord, You are my beloved.
May I live out the love You've poured out to me.
Empower me to do what You do:
      lovingly accept others,
      offer tenderness and grace,
      treat them with honor and dignity,
      hold them dear.
May I show them that Love is who You are,
and loved is what they are.

                          —C. M.

O God, in whom nothing can live but as it lives in love:
grant us the spirit of love,
which does not want to be rewarded, honored, or esteemed,
but only to become the blessing and happiness of all who
      need it;
this we pray in Your name, for You Yourself are Love.
      —WILLIAM LAW (1686–1761), ADAPTED

O God of Love, give us love:
love in our thinking,
love in our speaking,
love in our doing,
and love in the hidden places of our souls;
love of our neighbors near and far;
love of our friends, old and new;
love of those with whom we find it hard to bear,
and love of those who find it hard to bear with us;
love of those with whom we work,
and love of those with whom we take our ease;
love in joy, love in sorrow;
love in life, and love in death;
that so at length we may be worthy to dwell with You—
You who are eternal Love.

—WILLIAM TEMPLE (1881–1944)

Lord, direct my heart into Your love—
then help me keep myself in Your love.

—C. M.

May no shadow of my sin obscure
the sunshine of Your favor and love.

—JOHN MACDUFF (1818–1895)

PATIENCE

O blessed Jesus, give me stillness of soul in Thee.
Let Your mighty calmness reign in me;
Rule me, O King of gentleness, King of peace.
Give me control, great power of self-control,
control over my words, thoughts, and actions.
From all irritability, lack of meekness, lack of gentleness,
dear Lord, deliver me.
By Your own deep patience, give me patience.
Make me in this and all things more and more like You.

    —ST. JOHN OF THE CROSS (1542–1591)

Lord, give me humility as I remember that
You are patient with me.
Calm my heart
and lead me in kindness and gentleness.
Help me bear with the people around me in love—
remembering that love is patient and kind.
May I be quick to listen and slow to speak.
May I be like You:
slow to get angry,
full of grace and patience,
abounding in steadfast love and faithfulness.

    —C. M.

Give me a wise, patient, and courageous heart,
a soul full of devotion to serve You,
and strength against all temptations.
—WILLIAM LAUD (1573–1645), ADAPTED

Lord, direct my heart into
the steadfastness, endurance, and patience of Jesus.
—C. M.

O God, give us patience when those who are wicked
    hurt us.
O how impatient and angry we are
when we think ourselves unjustly slandered, reviled, and
    hurt! . . .
Grant us the virtue and patience, power and strength,
that we may take all adversity with goodwill,
and with a gentle mind overcome it.
And if necessity and honor require us to speak,
grant that we may do so with meekness and patience,
that the truth and Your glory may be defended.
—MILES COVERDALE (1488–1569)

PEACE

O Lord, calm the waves of this heart; calm its tempests!
Calm yourself, O my soul, so that divine can act in you!
Calm yourself, O my soul, so that God is able to repose
    in you,
so that His peace may cover you!
Yes, Father in heaven,
often have I found that the world cannot give me peace,
but make me feel that You are able to give me peace;
let me know the truth of Your promise:
that the world may not be able to take away Your peace.
—SØREN KIERKEGAARD (1813–1855)

Calm me, O Lord, as You stilled the storm.
Still me, O Lord; keep me from harm.
Let all the storms within me cease.
Enfold me, Lord, in Your peace.
—CELTIC PRAYER

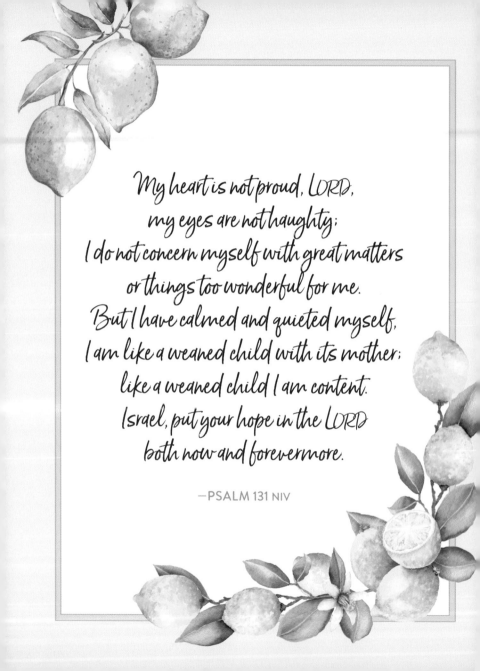

My heart is not proud, LORD,
my eyes are not haughty;
I do not concern myself with great matters
or things too wonderful for me.
But I have calmed and quieted myself,
I am like a weaned child with its mother;
like a weaned child I am content.
Israel, put your hope in the LORD
both now and forevermore.

—PSALM 131 NIV

You are the Lord of peace.
Come and fill my heart with Your peace—
that peace that comes only from You,
that goes beyond my understanding,
that You can provide at all times and in all situations.
I believe Your peace has the power
to trump everything around me and within me.
I put my hope in You.
May Your peace rule in me,
guarding my heart and mind,
as I live in You, Lord Jesus.

—C. M.

O Lord, lift up the light of Your countenance upon us;
let Your peace rule in our hearts,
and may it be our strength and our song. . . .
We commit ourselves to Your care and keeping.
Let Your grace be mighty in us,
and sufficient in us,
for all the duties of the day.

—MATTHEW HENRY (1662–1714)

God, help me identify what I'm allowing to rob me of
    peace:
        setbacks and disappointments,
        unanswered questions and unresolved issues,
        obstacles and others' behavior,
        my human limitations and vulnerabilities.
Grant me wisdom about where and how to spend my
    energy.
Help me accept what I can't control
and calmly persist in areas that are within my reach.
I rest in the fact that You are on the throne,
able to do all things,
and rejoice that Your Spirit is with me.
I turn over my concerns about the future to You
and embrace the gifts of the present moment with a
    contented heart.

                    —C. M.

Send Your peace into my heart, O Lord,
that I may be contented with the mercies of this day
and confident of Your protection for this night;
and having forgiven others,
even as You forgive me,
may I go to rest in tranquility and trust.

        —ST. FRANCIS OF ASSISI (1181–1226)

May Your holy angels lead us in the paths of peace and
goodwill.
May we be pardoned and forgiven for any sins and offenses.
May we be bound together by Your Holy Spirit . . . ,
entrusting one another and all our life to Christ.
—EASTERN ORTHODOX LITANY, ADAPTED

PROTECTION AND SAFETY

O Lord Jesus Christ,
who received the children who came to You,
receive also from me, Your child, this prayer.
Shelter me under the shadow of Your wings.
—ANONYMOUS

O God, with whom there is no darkness,
but the night shines as the day:
keep and defend us and all Your children . . .
throughout the coming night.
Renew our hearts with Your forgiveness
and our bodies with untroubled sleep,
that we may wake to use more faithfully Your gift of life.
—TRADITIONAL CATHOLIC PRAYER

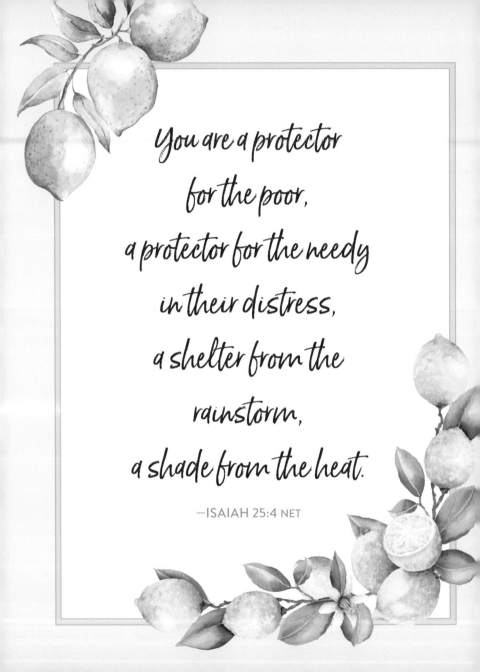

You are a protector
for the poor,
a protector for the needy
in their distress,
a shelter from the
rainstorm,
a shade from the heat.

—ISAIAH 25:4 NET

I pray You be very near to us all;
protect us by Your providential care over us,
and above all, surround us with Your love, power, and
    Spirit. . . .
Help us and we shall be helped;
keep us, and we shall be kept.
   —ELIZABETH FRY (1780–1845), ADAPTED

Continue your gracious protection to me, Lord, this
    night.
Defend me from all dangers,
and from the fear of them,
that I may enjoy such refreshing sleep
as may fit me for the duties of the coming day.
And grant me grace always to live so close to You . . .
that I may be completely Yours.
   —EDMUND GIBSON, BISHOP OF LONDON (1669–1748)

Abide with me, O good Lord,
through the night,
guarding, keeping, guiding, sustaining, sanctifying,
and with Your love gladdening me,
that in You I may ever live.
   —EDWARD WHITE BENSON (1829–1896)

Jesus Christ, my God, I adore You
and I thank You for all the graces
You have given me this day.
I offer You my sleep and all the moments of this night,
and I ask You to keep me safe from sin.
To this end I place myself in Your sacred side. . . .
Let Your holy angels surround me and keep me in peace;
and let Your blessing be upon me.

    —ST. ALPHONSUS LIGUORI (1696–1787)

Almighty God, to Your goodness
we commend ourselves this night,
asking Your protection of us
through its darkness and dangers.
We are helpless and dependent;
graciously preserve us.
We pray for everyone we love and value,
for every friend and connection,
however divided or far away.
We know that we are alike before You and under
    Your eye.
May we be equally united . . .
in fervent devotion to You
and in Your merciful protection.

    —JANE AUSTEN (1775–1817), ADAPTED

O Lord our God,
under the shadow of Your wings we will rest.
Defend and support us,
bear us up when we are little,
and we know that even down to our grey hairs
You will carry us.
    —ST. AUGUSTINE OF HIPPO (354–430)

O God, our heavenly Father,
whose glory fills the whole creation
and whose presence we find wherever we go:
Preserve those who travel . . . ;
surround them with Your loving care;
protect them from every danger;
and bring them in safety to their journey's end.
    —BOOK OF COMMON PRAYER

We call on You for those who travel:
graciously grant them an Angel of Peace
to be the companion of their way,
that they may not suffer any hurt at the hands of anyone,
that they may accomplish their travels
and their journeys in peace.
    —ST. SARAPION OF THMUIS (D. C. 362)

REST

Blessed be the God of love,
who gave me eyes and light and power
both to be busy and to play today. . . .
My God, You are all love.
Not one poor minute escapes You
but brings a favor from above.
And in this love,
more than in bed,
I rest.

—GEORGE HERBERT (1593–1633)

Give me this night, O Father,
the peace of mind that is truly rest.
Take from me . . . all resentment for anything
that has been withheld from me;
all foolish worry about the future
and all futile regret about the past.
Help me to be at peace with myself,
at peace with my fellow human beings,
at peace with You,
so indeed may I lay myself down to rest in peace,
through Jesus Christ my Lord.

—ANONYMOUS

O Father, come and rest Your children now. . . .
Remove from us the weight of our heavy armor for a while,
and may we just have peace,
perfect peace,
and be at rest.
—CHARLES SPURGEON (1834–1892)

O God, in the course of this busy life,
give us times of refreshment and peace;
and grant that we may so use our leisure
to rebuild our bodies and renew our minds,
that our spirits may be opened to
the goodness of Your creation.
—BOOK OF COMMON PRAYER

O Lord God, You have given us the night for rest. . . .
As I lay aside my cares to relax and relieve my mind,
may I not forget your infinite and unresting care for me.
And in this way, let my conscience be at peace,
so that when I rise tomorrow,
I will be refreshed in body, mind, and soul.
—JOHN CALVIN (1509–1564)

Lord Jesus Christ, You are the source of all peace,
reconciling the whole universe to the Father.
You are the source of all rest,
calming troubled hearts,
and bringing sleep to weary bodies.
You are the sweetness that fills our minds with quiet joy
and can turn the worst nightmares into dreams of heaven.
May I dream of Your sweetness,
rest in Your arms,
be at one with Your Father,
and be comforted in the knowledge
that You always watch over me.
    —ERASMUS OF ROTTERDAM (C. 1466–1536)

O Lord, support us all the day long,
until the shadows lengthen,
and the evening comes,
and the busy world is hushed,
and the fever of life is over,
and our work is done.
Then, in your mercy,
give us safe lodging,
a holy rest,
and peace at last.
    —ST. JOHN HENRY NEWMAN (1801–1890)

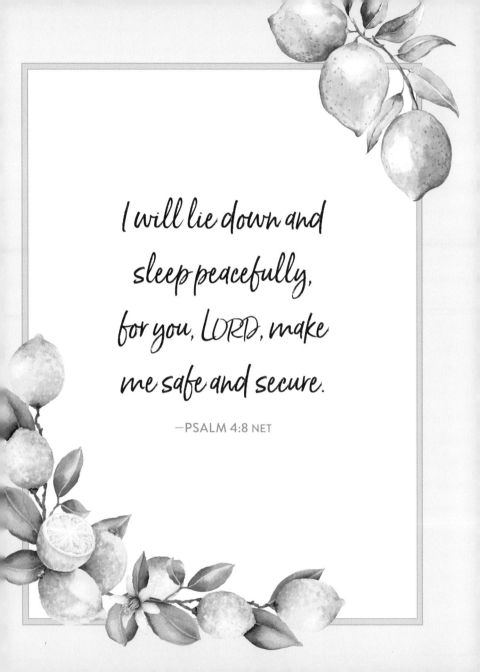

I will lie down and
sleep peacefully,
for you, LORD, make
me safe and secure.

—PSALM 4:8 NET

Now the light goes away.
Savior, listen while I pray,
Asking You to watch and keep
And to send me quiet sleep.
Jesus, Savior, wash away
All that has been wrong today.
Help me every day to be
Good and gentle, more like Thee. . . .
Now my evening praise I give:
You did die that I might live.
All my blessings come for Thee.
Oh how good You are to me!
—FRANCES RIDLEY HAVERGAL (1836–1879)

Good Jesus, strength of the weary,
rest of the restless,
by the weariness and unrest of Your sacred cross,
come to me who am weary
that I may rest in You.
—EDWARD BOUVERIE PUSEY (1800–1882)

STRENGTH

Lord, flood my heart with Your light
so I may see the magnificent works You're doing
and have confident hope in You.
Help me grasp the immensity
of the gifts and power You have for me.
From Your glorious, unlimited resources,
give me inner strength.
May the power You used
to raise Jesus from the dead
and to set Him on the throne of the universe
be alive and at work in me now.
Energize and embolden me
to carry out every good thing
You've prepared for me to do.

—C. M.

O God, You are the light of the minds that know You,
the life of the souls that love You,
and the strength of the wills that serve You.

—ST. AUGUSTINE OF HIPPO (354–430)

God, You know my struggle.
You know my weariness.
You know my weakness.
Instead of denying it
or letting the discouragement of it swallow me,
I lift my eyes up . . .
My help comes from You.
You say that . . .

> those who trust in You will receive new strength;
> Your power works perfectly in my weakness;
> Your grace is big enough to meet my
>   immense need;
> You can strengthen me to do anything You want
>   me to do.

And I believe You.
So I bow before You, God Most High,
ready to receive You as my all in all,
ready to honor You by depending on You.
Come make me strong in Your strength!
Increase my capacity so I can take on what's in front of me.
Creator God, create something new in me—
whatever pleases You most.
Come with Your might
and make Your power work through me
so my life will be full of Your glory.

—C. M.

Go with each of us to rest. . . .
When the day returns, return to us,
our sun and comforter,
and call us up with morning faces and with morning
      hearts,
eager to labor,
eager to be happy,
if happiness should be our portion,
and if the day is marked for sorrow,
strong to endure it.
    —ROBERT LOUIS STEVENSON (1850–1894),
      WRITTEN THE NIGHT BEFORE HE DIED

God, I commit myself to Your care through Christ.
Forgive me for all my sins of this day.
Keep Your grace alive in my heart
and cleanse me from all pride, harshness, and selfishness.
Give me a spirit of meekness, humility, steadiness,
      and love.
Keep Yourself ever present to me
and perfect Your strength in my weakness.
Take me and those I love under Your blessed care.
    —THOMAS ARNOLD (1795–1842), ADAPTED

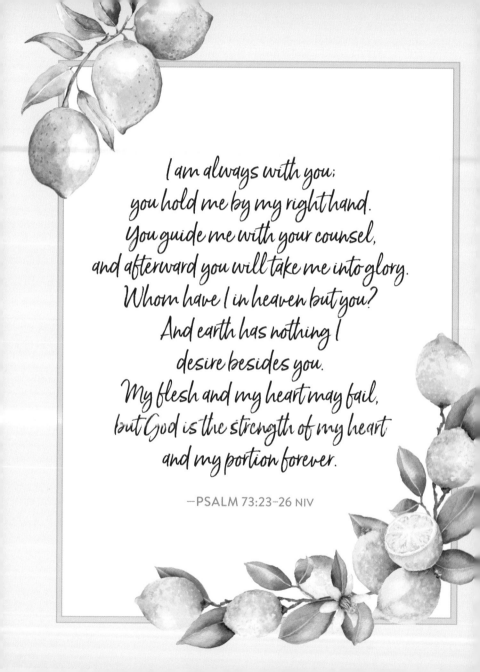

I am always with you;
you hold me by my right hand.
You guide me with your counsel,
and afterward you will take me into glory.
Whom have I in heaven but you?
And earth has nothing I
desire besides you.
My flesh and my heart may fail,
but God is the strength of my heart
and my portion forever.

—PSALM 73:23–26 NIV

O Lord my God, my one hope, . . .
give me strength to seek You,
as You have made me to find You,
and given me hope of finding You ever more and more.
My strength and weakness are in Your hands:
preserve the one, and remedy the other. . . .
Let me remember You, understand You, love You.
Increase in me all these
until You restore me to Your perfect pattern.

—ST. AUGUSTINE OF HIPPO (354–430)

WILLINGNESS TO FORGIVE

Lord, grant that anger
or other bitterness
does not reign over us,
but that by Your grace,
genuine kindness,
loyalty,
and every kind of friendliness,
generosity,
and gentleness
may reign in us.

—MARTIN LUTHER (1483–1546)

Give us, O Lord, a humble spirit,
that we . . . may always live
as those who have been forgiven much.
Make us tender and compassionate
toward those who are overtaken by temptation,
considering ourselves,
how we have fallen in times past and may fall yet again.
Make us watchful and sober-minded,
looking ever to You for grace to do what is right.
　　—CHARLES JOHN VAUGHAN (1816–1897)

Lord, You are gentle and kind,
full of compassion and grace.
You patiently bear with me
and offer me undeserved, unconditional love
all the time.
Fill me with Your Spirit
so I may do the same toward others.
Help me see them the way You do,
with eyes of love.
Make me eager to show them Your heart
and seek their good.
　　　　　　—C. M.

O Lord Jesus, because, being full of foolishness,
we often sin and have to ask pardon,
help us to forgive as we would be forgiven;
neither mentioning old offenses committed against us,
nor dwelling upon them in thought,
nor being influenced by them in heart;
but loving our brother freely, as You freely loved us.
—CHRISTINA ROSSETTI (1830–1894)

Take away, O Lord, from our hearts
all suspicion, indignation, anger, contention,
and whatever is calculated to wound charity
and to lessen brotherly love.
—THOMAS À KEMPIS (1380–1471)

Save me from cherishing my wounds
and being controlled by my emotions.
Help me remember that holding grudges
won't bring peace or wholeness;
only You can do that.
I entrust my heart to You:
mend what is damaged, heal what is broken.
Then help me move on,
forgetting past frustrations and offenses,
walking in the lightness of freedom and joy.
—C. M.

Six

Prayers for When You're Struggling

If we want to see mighty wonders of divine power and grace wrought in the place of weakness, failure, and disappointment, let us answer God's standing challenge, "Call unto Me, and I will answer you, and show you great and mighty things, which you do not know."

—HUDSON TAYLOR

The challenges of life have the power to knock us over. Then the discouragement of our struggles can sink us into despair.

But the Bible's repeated message is: Don't be surprised by difficulty. Difficulty itself is not the enemy; walking through it alone, apart from God, is the real danger to avoid.

Difficulties are opportunities for transformation when we combine them with prayer. They can stretch our faith, build our dependence on God, bring the Spirit's empowerment, and develop our ability to have peace in any situation.

We can begin by coming to God as a bundle of pain, consumed with our problems and burdens. He will receive us with compassion and hold us. And in His presence, our perspective will shift.

We'll realize He is greater than everything we're facing and everything we're feeling. We'll put our faith in His character and power. Uniting ourselves with Him, and then moving forward with Him, will give us the ability to handle our hardest moments.

The goal is to remain in that connection. Like Peter walking on the water toward Jesus, when our focus turns to our problems or fear, we'll sink. But when we give Him our attention, we'll see Him as more powerful than everything else that threatens us. We will move in His strength and be transformed in the process.

Ephesians 3 says, "God can do anything, you know—far more than you could ever imagine or guess or request in your wildest dreams! He does it not by pushing us around but by working within us, his Spirit deeply and gently within us" (vv. 20–21 THE MESSAGE).

We may ask God to take the burden away or give us the ability to endure it. He may throw open the jail cell or miraculously heal. Or He may allow the hardship. As we submit to God's wisdom, we trust that, however He leads, He is doing holy work through His master plan. We know every struggle is worthwhile.

CHALLENGES

Give me, O Lord, patience and a sense of purpose
in each of the things that challenge me. . . .
Protect me through the dangers and confusion of life on
    earth. . . .
Fix my trust, my timid hopes, upon Yourself,
so that I may stand on a secure foundation.
Lift up my thoughts with Your wisdom.
    —*THE EXETER BOOK* (C. 950), ADAPTED

I know that when the stress has grown too strong,
You will be there.
I know that when the waiting seems so long,
You hear my prayer.
I know that through the crash of falling worlds
You're holding me.
I know that life and death are Yours eternally.
    —JANET ERSKINE STUART (1857–1914)

Save us from . . . unbelief.
In pressing difficulties,
how ready we are to distrust Your goodness!
How hard we find it to rely upon Your Word
and Your invisible power!
May we receive Your promises in the full assurance of
     faith
and wait for the accomplishment of them in hope,
though all things seem to go contrary to them.
—HENRY VENN OF THE CLAPHAM SECT (1725–1797)

Dear Lord and Savior, Jesus Christ,
I hold up all my weakness to Your strength,
my failure to Your faithfulness,
my sinfulness to Your perfection,
my loneliness to Your compassion,
my little pains to Your great agony on the Cross.
I pray that You will cleanse me, strengthen me, and
     hide me,
so that, in all ways, my life may be lived
as You would have it lived,
without cowardice and for You alone.
          —JANET ERSKINE STUART (1857–1914)

God, by Your loving providence,
sorrows, difficulties, trials, and dangers
become means of grace,
lessons of patience,
and channels of hope.
Grant us the good will to use these privileges.
　—CHRISTINA ROSSETTI (1830–1894), ADAPTED

Jesus, You are my true friend. . . .
You take part in all my misfortunes;
You take them on yourself.
You know how to change them into blessings.
You listen to me with the greatest kindness
when I relate my troubles to You,
and You always have balm to pour on my wounds.
I find You at all times,
I find You everywhere,
I find You wherever I go.
You are never weary of listening to me.
You are never tired of doing me good.
　—ST. CLAUDE LA COLOMBIÈRE (1641–1682)

CHANGE

It is well and good, Lord,
if all things change,
provided we are rooted in You.
       —ST. JOHN OF THE CROSS (1542–1591)

Help me to accept that change is part of life,
to welcome the newness each change brings,
and to embrace the gifts and joys of each season.
I trust Your guiding hand, God.
Help me adapt and
have a willing, adventurous spirit.
May I look for the valuable opportunities
You're giving me in this situation
and make the most of them.
May I say yes to wherever You lead,
being glad and grateful to be on
a journey of discovery and growth with You.
       —C. M.

Lord, I am disoriented and unsettled in the midst of
   change.
Steady my heart and be my constant.
I thank You for Your word to me:
      "The mountains may move and the hills disappear,
      but even then my faithful love for you will remain."
Surround me now with Your unfailing love.
You are my refuge, my strong tower, my foundation.
You are my heart's home forever,
no matter where I am or what happens around me.
Help me sense Your nearness, guidance, and love
throughout this season of change,
and may I grow closer to You as I depend on You more.
—C. M., QUOTED MATERIAL FROM ISAIAH 54:10 NLT

Be present, O merciful God, and protect me. . . .
As I am fatigued by the changes
and the chances of this fleeting world,
I rest in Your eternal changelessness;
through Jesus Christ,
who is the same yesterday, today, and forever.
      —LEONINE SACRAMENTARY (5TH C.)

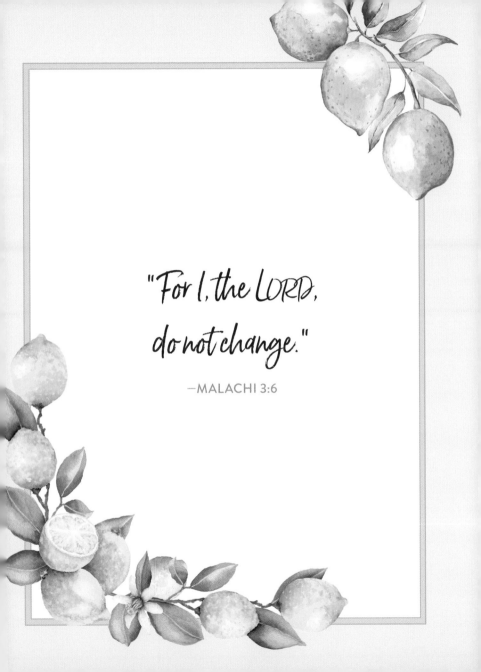

"For I, the LORD,
do not change."

—MALACHI 3:6

DEPRESSION

Lord, my prayers are dead,
my affections dead,
and my heart is dead:
but You are a living God
and I commit myself to You.

    —WILLIAM BRIDGE (C. 1600–1670)

Everything seems dull,
every action feels like a burden.
If anyone speaks, I scarcely listen. . . .
My heart is as hard as flint.
Then I go out into the field to meditate,
to read the holy Scriptures,
and I write down my deepest thoughts in a letter
    to You.
And suddenly Your grace, dear Jesus,
shatters the darkness with daylight,
lifts the burden,
relieves the tension.
Soon tears follow sighs,
and heavenly joy floods over me.

    —ST. AELRED OF RIEVAULX (C. 1110–1167)

God, stretch out Your strong arm
and pull me out of this pit I find myself in,
one of self-absorption and self-pity.
With Your mighty power,
move me out of the dark shadows
of melancholy and despair
and into the fresh air and sunshine of hope and love.
Help me to feel Your love
through the people who care about me.
Show me how I can serve someone else
and find joy in meeting their needs.
Remind me of Your great works
and stir my heart to worship You.
Give me a song of praise I can sing
as I put my trust in You.
Pull me into the current of Your living water
and revive in me a great energy for life.
Open my eyes to the delights that surround me,
and fill my heart with dreams
of what sweet and fulfilling moments may lie ahead.
Guide me in doing the good works You created me to do,
in filling my role in Your great purposes.
Bring me alive in Your joy, and help me inhabit Your love.

—C. M.

O God, we thank You for this earth, our home;
for the wide sky and the blessed sun,
for the salt sea and the running water,
for the everlasting hills and the never-resting winds,
for trees and the grass underfoot.
We thank You for our senses
by which we hear the songs of birds,
and see the splendor of the summer fields,
and taste of the autumn fruits,
and rejoice in the feel of the snow,
and smell the breath of the spring.
Grant us a heart wide open to all this beauty,
and save our souls from being so blind
that we pass unseeing
when even the common thornbush
is aflame with Your glory,
O God our creator,
who lives and reigns forever and ever!
    —WALTER RAUSCHENBUSCH (1861–1918)

Father, I ask that You lift me out of this darkness
and help me be present to the light that surrounds me.
    —C. M.

O God, You made me for Yourself,
to show forth Your goodness in me.
Reveal the life-giving power of Your holy nature
    within me;
guide me to a true and living faith in You,
to strongly hunger and thirst after
the birth, life, and spirit of Your holy Jesus in my soul.
May all that is within me be turned from
every inward thought
or outward work that is not of You,
to Your holy Jesus and heavenly workings in my soul.
    —WILLIAM LAW (1686–1761), ADAPTED

Lord, help me to glorify You by contentment. . . .
I have talents; help me to extol You by spending them
    for You.
I have time; help me to redeem it, that I may serve You.
I have a heart to feel; let it feel no love but Yours.
I have a head to think; help me to think of You and
    for You.
You have put me in this world for something, Lord.
Show me what that is, and help me work out my life
    purpose.
    —CHARLES SPURGEON (1834–1892)

DOUBT

I am an empty vessel that needs to be filled.
My Lord, fill it.
I am weak in the faith;
strengthen me.
I am cold in love;
warm me and make me fervent
that my love may go out to my neighbor.
I do not have a strong and firm faith;
at times I doubt and am unable to trust You altogether.
O Lord, help me.
Strengthen my faith and trust in You.

—MARTIN LUTHER (1483–1546)

To you, O Jesus, peace of the troubled heart, I come!
Save me from myself.
Shine into my heart with Your life and love.
Melt away all cold distrust.
Take away all sin
and make me like You,
for Your love and kindness' sake!

—WILLIAM BOYD CARPENTER (1841–1918)

While faith is with me, I am blest;
It turns my darkest night to day;
But while I clasp it to my breast,
I often feel it slide away. . . .
Oh, help me, God! For You alone
Can my distracted soul relieve;
Forsake it not: it is Your own,
Though weak, yet longing to believe.
Oh, drive these cruel doubts away;
And make me know that You are God!
A faith, that shines by night and day,
Will lighten every earthly load.
If I believe that Jesus died,
And, waking, rose to reign above;
Then surely sorrow, sin, and pride,
Must yield to peace, and hope, and love.
And all the blessed words He said
Will strength and holy joy impart:
A shield of safety o'er my head,
A spring of comfort in my heart.

—ANNE BRONTË (1820–1849)

Save me, O Lord, from the snares of a double mind;
deliver me from all cowardly neutralities.
Make me to go in the path of your commandments,
and to trust for my defense in Your mighty arm alone.

—RICHARD HURRELL FROUDE (1803–1836)

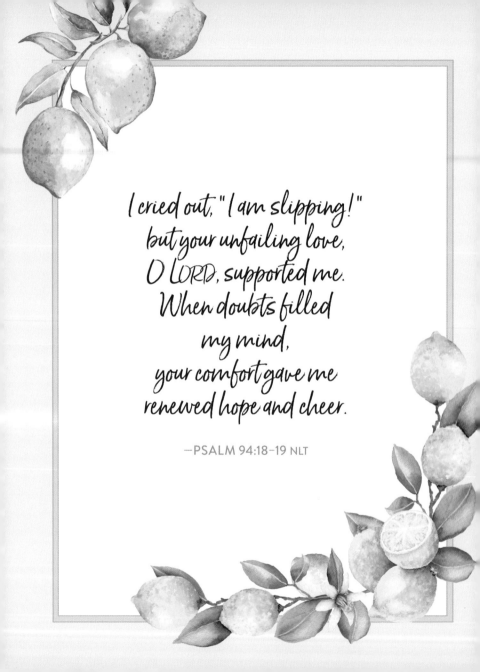

I cried out, "I am slipping!"
but your unfailing love,
O LORD, supported me.
When doubts filled
my mind,
your comfort gave me
renewed hope and cheer.

—PSALM 94:18–19 NLT

FEAR AND ANXIETY

Son of God, who subdued the troubled waters
and laid to rest the fears of men,
let Your majesty master us and
Your power of calm control us.
Replace our fears with faith
and our unrest with perfect trust in You,
who lives and governs all things, world without end.
—JOHN WALLACE SUTER (1859–1942), ADAPTED

Set free, O Lord, the souls of Your servants
from all restlessness and anxiety.
Give us that peace and power which flow from You.
Keep us in all perplexity and distress,
that upheld by Your strength
and stayed on the rock of Your faithfulness,
we may abide in You now and forevermore.
—FRANCIS PAGET (1851–1911)

To You alone, O Jesus, I must cling;
running to Your arms, dear Lord,
there let me hide, safe from all fears,
loving You with the tenderness of a child.

— ST. THÉRÈSE OF LISIEUX (1873–1897)

You say that if I give You my burdens,
You will take care of me.
You say that I should cast all my cares upon You,
  because You love me,
  because You can handle them all,
  and because it shows my faith in You.
A burden that is heavy enough to sink me
is as light as a feather to You.
A fear that can paralyze me
has no power over You.
So I unload it all before You
and hand it over for You to manage.
I put my trust in You—not in my perspective or resources.
You can do anything, God!
I will not be afraid, because You are my King and Father.
You are with me, and You are for me.
You accept me as I need You and rely on You,
and You walk with me now and always.
You will strengthen me for whatever comes.

— C. M.

Lord, my emotions could propel me downward
or pull a curtain around me, blocking Your light.
But instead, I look to You and pray:
Train my mind on Your truth.
Shape my thoughts with Your Spirit.
Fill my heart with Your peace.
Guide me and give me self-control to do what is wise.
I trust that what You say is more real than what I feel.

—C. M.

Make my body healthy and agile,
my mind sharp and clear,
my heart joyful and contented,
my soul faithful and loving. . . .
Above all let me live in Your presence,
for with You all fear is banished
and there is only harmony and peace.
Let every day combine the beauty of spring,
the brightness of summer,
the abundance of autumn,
and the repose of winter.
And at the end of my life on earth,
grant that I may come to see and know You
in the fullness of Your glory.

—ST. THOMAS AQUINAS (1225–1274)

Everything I could be worrying about right now,
I'm praying about instead.
My concerns could take over my mind all day
and seize my heart with despair.
But instead I'm taking those thoughts captive
and turning to You.
I want to make my mind obedient to You, the Truth.
I tell You what I need and hope for,
then let the matters rest in Your hands.
I rejoice that I belong to You, and You are a good Father.
You've provided before, and You will again.
I realize my situation is an exercise in faith-training,
an opportunity to trust You and give You glory.
Now, Holy Spirit, the Great Helper,
give me self-control throughout this day
and help me fix my thoughts where You want them.
May I find the good all around me.
May I fill my mind with what's right and pure—
"the best, not the worst; the beautiful, not the ugly;
things to praise, not things to curse."
May I dwell on—and give power to—what is true.
May I find even simple things to delight in.
Help me choose joy; choose hope; choose peace.

—C. M., QUOTED MATERIAL

FROM PHILIPPIANS 4:8 THE MESSAGE

Most loving Father,
who has taught us to dread nothing but the loss of You,
preserve me from faithless fears and worldly anxieties.
—WILLIAM BRIGHT (1824–1901)

O my Lord and Savior,
in Your arms I am safe.
Keep me and I have nothing to fear. . . .
I know nothing about the future,
but I rely upon You.
I pray that You would give me what is good for me. . . .
If You bring pain or sorrow on me,
give me grace to bear it well—
keep me from fretfulness and selfishness.
If You give me health and strength and success in this world,
keep me always on my guard
lest these great gifts carry me away from You.
O Christ, You died on the Cross for me,
even for me, sinner as I am.
Help me to know You,
to believe in You,
to love You,
to serve You,
to always aim at bringing You glory,
to live to and for You.
—ST. JOHN HENRY NEWMAN (1801–1890)

ILLNESS

Almighty God,
You are the only source of health and healing
and the only true peace in the universe.
Bring Your Spirit of calmness.
Give us an awareness of Your presence
and perfect confidence in You.
In all pain and weariness and anxiety,
may we throw ourselves upon Your protecting care,
where we are fenced in and surrounded by Your loving
    power.
Give us strength and peace
and restore our health.

—HENRY BLAUVELT WILSON (1870–1923),

ADAPTED

May the healing power of our risen Lord, Jesus Christ,
fill your whole being, body, mind, and spirit.
May He take away all that hurts or harms you,
and give you His peace.

—ANONYMOUS

Lord, my body is hurting.
My mind is troubled.
My heart is discouraged.
I am so very aware of my human state before You:
vulnerable and in need.
Just as You first made me, remake me now.
Just as You first brought me to life, revitalize me now.
Just as You have healed my heart and body
from other wounds throughout my life, heal me now.
As the One who created me, preserve me.
Mend, renew, and strengthen Your workmanship.
In Your love and tenderness, come and make me whole,
body, mind, and spirit,
for Your mercy's sake.

—C. M.

We call on You for those that are sick;
graciously grant them health,
raise them from sickness,
and give them perfect health of body and soul.
For You are the Healer and Benefactor.
You are the Lord and King of all.

—ST. SARAPION OF THMUIS (D. C. 362)

Jesus, the Healer, I come to You in great faith.
I reach out to touch You, even only the hem of Your
    garment.
I know nothing is too hard for You,
and I ask Your limitless power to meet my need.
Because You are good, take care of me and make me well.

                    —C. M.

Lord, I trust You;
use me, whatever and wherever I am.
If I am sick, may my sickness serve You;
if I am sorrowful, may my sorrow serve You.
Lord, You know what You are about.
I trust You.
Thanks be to God.

        —ST. JOHN HENRY NEWMAN (1801–1890),
                    ADAPTED

Lord, grant me the gift of patience when I am well,
so that I may use it when I am sick.
When I am healthy, and relying on myself alone,
I often discover how weak I am.
Help me, when I am ill, to find the strength
which comes from depending solely on You.

        —THOMAS FULLER (1608–1661), ADAPTED

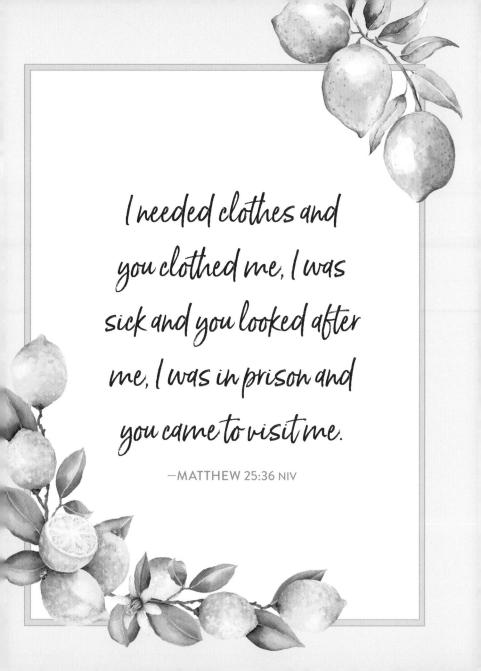

I needed clothes and
you clothed me, I was
sick and you looked after
me, I was in prison and
you came to visit me.

—MATTHEW 25:36 NIV

Almighty God, Father of all mercies,
who has promised to be with Your children always;
look upon those who suffer
and are sorely in need of Your help
through illness of body, mind, or spirit.
Lift us up to Your presence, dear Lord,
that we may with faith move forward.
Give us such a measure of hope
that it will continually sustain us.
And if it be Your will, grant to us new health,
release from our illness,
and peace of mind.
Help us to know, above all,
that having surrendered ourselves to You,
we are in Your loving arms.
Keep us safe, dear Lord, with You,
ever mindful of Him who suffered,
teaching us a new meaning of pain,
Your Son, Jesus Christ our Lord,
who lived and died for us.
In His Spirit and in sure confidence,
we offer this, our imperfect prayer.

—THOMAS H. WRIGHT (1873–1928)

LONELINESS

Jesus, in Your great loneliness on the Mount of Olives,
and in Your agony,
You prayed to Your heavenly Father for comfort.
You know that there are souls on earth
who are without support and without comforters.
Send them an angel to give them joy.

—ANONYMOUS

Father God, You sought me and adopted me,
bringing me into Your realm of love.
I am in Your mighty and steadfast care.
I am in Your unconditional and constant love.
Even when my family forsakes me, You receive me.
Even when my friends disappoint me, You remain
    with me.
When I feel like I'm falling, You hold me up.
When I feel like a lost cause, You accept me.
My kind Father, help me remember
that Your love is strong,
and that nothing will ever separate me from You.

—C. M.

Father, let me hold Your hand
and like a child walk with You down all my days,
secure in Your love and strength.

—THOMAS À KEMPIS (1380–1471)

Lord, You are closer to me than my own breathing,
nearer than my hands and feet.

—ST. TERESA OF ÁVILA (1515–1582)

Be O Lord,
a guiding star above me,
a smooth path below me,
a kindly shepherd behind me
and a bright flame before me;
today, tonight, and forever.
Alone with none but You, my God,
I journey on my way.
What need I fear, when You are near
O King of night and day?
More safe am I within Your hand,
Than if a host did round me stand.

—ST. COLUMBA OF IRELAND (C. 521–597)

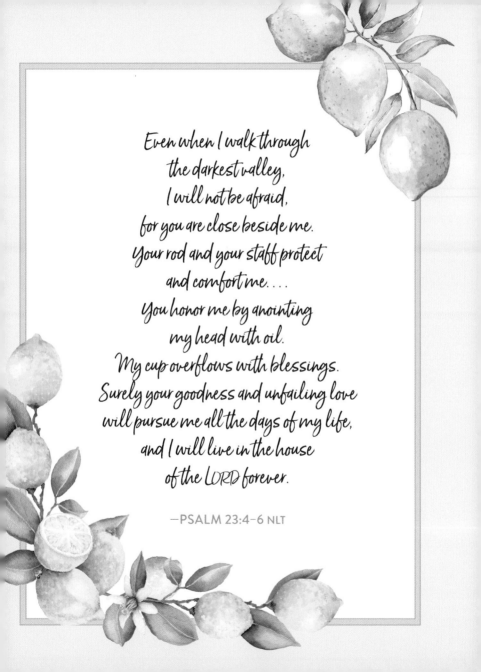

Even when I walk through
the darkest valley,
I will not be afraid,
for you are close beside me.
Your rod and your staff protect
and comfort me. . . .
You honor me by anointing
my head with oil.
My cup overflows with blessings.
Surely your goodness and unfailing love
will pursue me all the days of my life,
and I will live in the house
of the LORD forever.

—PSALM 23:4–6 NLT

LOSS

Lord Jesus, You are my light in the darkness.
You are my warmth in the cold.
You are my happiness in sorrow.

—ANONYMOUS

Lord, You hear Your people
when they call to You for help,
and help them in their trouble.
You rescue those whose spirits are crushed
and comfort those who mourn.
I feel shattered and empty, consumed by my pain.
Find me in the darkness and hold me close to Your heart.
I know You are able to carry me through anything.
Give me hope that things will get better,
and that You will heal me and make me whole.
Make me patient and able to endure this pain.
Help me not to be overwhelmed and paralyzed.
Help me take my next step in Your strength.

—C. M.

I have lost everything. . . .
O friend of my heart,
O my good and devout husband,
you are dead and have left me in misery.
How will I live without you? . . .
May He who does not forsake widows and orphans
    console me.
O my God, console me!
O my Jesus, strengthen me in my weakness!
   —ST. ELIZABETH OF HUNGARY (1207–1231)

Lord God, make me strong and of good courage.
All the beauty of our past life together, the home we made,
the dignity and glory of it,
the fellowship, the humor, the conspiracies, the discussions,
the . . . pulsating life,
the splendid web You gave us to weave—
all this is over.
With one touch You called him home,
and it has fallen to pieces around me.
Give me strength and power to be still and see what You
    will do.
   —MARY BENSON (1841–1918), WRITTEN AFTER
THE DEATH OF HER HUSBAND, ARCHBISHOP OF
CANTERBURY EDWARD WHITE BENSON, IN 1896

Most merciful God,
whose wisdom is beyond our understanding,
deal graciously with _____ in their grief.
Surround them with Your love,
that they may not be overwhelmed by their loss,
but have confidence in Your goodness,
and strength to meet the days to come.

—BOOK OF COMMON PRAYER

Lord, meet me in my grief.
Put Your loving arms around me
and help me sense Your nearness.
Help me to accept my feelings
rather than trying to escape them.
My emotions seem overwhelming in their power,
but I will not forget that You are greater than all things.
Hold my feelings, God,
and lead me through this unfamiliar place.
Thank You that You will stay with me,
hour after hour,
and provide for the great needs of my soul.
Bring me Your comfort,
Your strength,
and Your peace that goes beyond understanding.
Be my all in all.

—C. M.

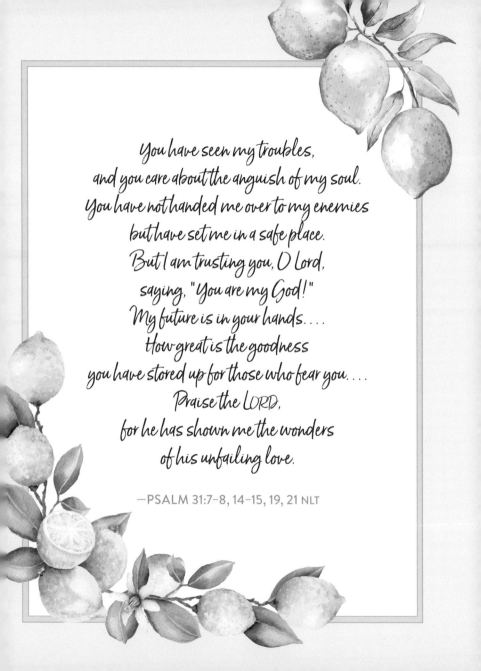

You have seen my troubles,
and you care about the anguish of my soul.
You have not handed me over to my enemies
but have set me in a safe place.
But I am trusting you, O Lord,
saying, "You are my God!"
My future is in your hands....
How great is the goodness
you have stored up for those who fear you....
Praise the LORD,
for he has shown me the wonders
of his unfailing love.

—PSALM 31:7–8, 14–15, 19, 21 NLT

SUFFERING

The horrors of darkness were gathered around me
and covered me all over,
and I saw no way to go forth. . . .
It was heavier than I could bear,
and I was crushed down under it. . . .
But in the depths of misery, O Lord,
I remembered that You are all-powerful,
that I had called You Father,
and I felt that I loved You.
I was made quiet in Your will,
and I waited for Your deliverance.
You had pity on me when no one else could help me.
I saw meekness under suffering in the example of
    Your Son,
and You taught me to follow Him,
saying, "Your will, O Father, be done!"
    —JOHN WOOLMAN (1720–1772), ADAPTED

Lord, show me more of who You are
and make me who You want me to become
through this season of suffering.
    —C. M.

As the rain hides the stars,
as the autumn mist hides the hills,
as the clouds veil the blue of the sky,
so the dark happenings of my life
hide the shining of Your face from me.
Yet, if I may hold Your hand in the darkness,
it is enough.
Since I know that—
though I may stumble in my going—
You do not fall.

—GAELIC PRAYER

Almighty and ever-living God,
in Your tender love for the human race,
You sent Your Son our Savior Jesus Christ
to take upon Him our nature,
and to suffer death upon the cross,
giving us the example of His great humility.
Mercifully grant that we may
walk in the way of His suffering,
and also share in His resurrection.

—GELASIAN SACRAMENTARY (8TH C.)

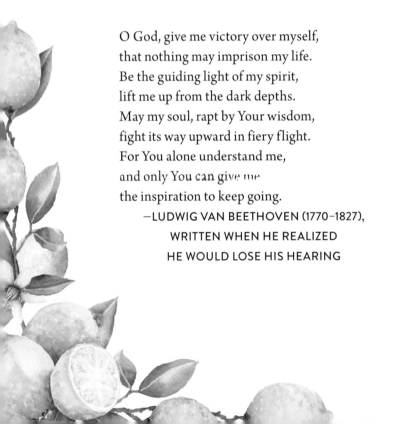

Even though I feel wrecked,
even though my world is falling apart,
may I look for reasons to sing
and ways to worship You.
Shine a light on Your goodness and beauty
all around me.
Fill my heart with hope and praise and courage.

—C. M.

O God, give me victory over myself,
that nothing may imprison my life.
Be the guiding light of my spirit,
lift me up from the dark depths.
May my soul, rapt by Your wisdom,
fight its way upward in fiery flight.
For You alone understand me,
and only You can give me
the inspiration to keep going.

—LUDWIG VAN BEETHOVEN (1770–1827),
WRITTEN WHEN HE REALIZED
HE WOULD LOSE HIS HEARING

TEMPTATION

Rule over me this day, O God,
leading me on the path of righteousness.
Put Your Word in my mind and Your truth in my heart,
that this day I neither think nor feel anything except
what is good and honest. . . .
Let my eyes always look straight ahead
on the road You wish me to tread,
that I might not be tempted by any distraction.
—JACOB BOEHME (1575–1624)

O God, by Your mercy strengthen us
who lie exposed to the rough storms
of troubles and temptations.
Help us against our own negligence and cowardice,
and defend us from the treachery of our unfaithful
hearts.
Help us and bring us to Your safe haven of peace.
—ST. AUGUSTINE OF HIPPO (354–430)

Lord, part of me wants what You want,
and part of me wrestles with
the broken desires of my sinful heart.
Meet me in this place of inner conflict.
Keep showing me a way out
of the temptation trap every time it comes up.
Help me remember:
You're not telling me to attempt something
no one else has done.
No temptation I face is beyond
what others have had to deal with
throughout the centuries.
And You're not telling me to do anything
I can't do in Your strength.
You'll never allow any temptation to be
more than I can stand—with Your help.
In my moments of struggle,
help me push against and turn away from
what is bad for my soul and dishonoring to You.
Prompt me to chase after what is
pure, lovely, and good instead.
Help me endure those moments
in Your strength, my faithful God.

—C. M.

O Lord, shield of our help,
who will not let us be tempted
beyond what we are able,
help us in all our wrestling
to lift up our eyes to You
and keep our hearts turned toward You.

—CHRISTINA ROSSETTI (1830–1894),
ADAPTED

Fix the center of my heart in Yourself, O Lord.
For only with You
will I resist temptation
and live according to Your will.

—MEISTER ECKHART (C. 1260–C. 1327),
ADAPTED

Let my conscience be clear,
my conduct without fault,
my speech blameless,
my life well-ordered.
Put me on guard against my human weaknesses.
Let me cherish Your love for me.

—POPE CLEMENT XI (1649–1721)

Lord, help me guard against laziness
and giving in to what is easy
or feels good in the moment.
May my love for You overcome my weakness,
and may my desire to walk with You in the light
propel me toward right living.
May I follow my Lord Jesus in His perfect example
of resisting temptation
and treasuring You above anything else.
Help me stay alert to triggers and warning signs
that temptation is near.
Keep me from wandering into dangerous territory
without realizing it.
Through Your Holy Spirit,
give me mastery over my impulses
and wisdom in my choices.
Prompt me to stop myself before I do anything I regret
and to remove myself from temptation

—C. M.

Give me a tender conscience,
that I may flee from all evil.

—HENRY THORNTON (1760–1815)

Lord, for our sake You fought
and overcame the temptations in the wilderness.
I pray that I may have the strength
to fight against our enemy the devil.
Be with me today in my thoughts and plans.
—ANGLICAN CHURCH OF PAPUA NEW GUINEA

Breathe in me, Holy Spirit, that I may think what is holy.
Move me, Holy Spirit, that I may do what is holy.
Attract me, Holy Spirit, that I may love what is holy.
Strengthen me, Holy Spirit, that I may guard what
        is holy.
Guard me, Holy Spirit, that I may keep what is holy.
        —ST. AUGUSTINE OF HIPPO (354-430)

Lift up our hearts, O Christ,
above the false show of things,
above laziness and fear,
above selfishness and covetousness,
above whim and fashion,
up to the everlasting Truth that you are;
that we may live joyfully and freely,
in the faith that You are our King and our Savior.
        —CHARLES KINGSLEY (1819-1875)

Seven

Prayers for Specific Life Events and Celebrations

Prayer brings to us blessings which we need, and
which only God can give, and which prayer can
alone convey to us. . . . Prayer is simply asking
God to do for us what He has promised us He
will do if we ask Him.

—GERHARD TERSTEEGEN

A s we abide with God, we welcome Him into every area
and every season of our lives. This can mean literal seasons
throughout the year and new personal seasons—including those
transitional times of endings and new beginnings. This collection
of prayers will guide you in walking with Him during some of life's
most significant events.

A precious person has arrived, born new to the world, and we're exploding with joy and overtaken with wonder.

We must say good-bye to someone whose time on earth has come to a close, and our hearts are heavy.

We have the honor of participating in a sacrament, which ushers us into a holy encounter. In these moments we want to open our hearts to God and experience Him as fully as we can.

We embark on a brand-new beginning, or we hit a landmark that prompts reflection on God's faithfulness and kindness to us in the past.

God has blessings that are suited for each of these moments. Throughout every high and low, He wants us to be present to Him, building intimacy with Him and depending on His perfect provision. He also invites us to be a blessing in the lives of others and witness the miracle of fellowship. Prayer is the perfect way to be unified together during these sacred events.

In special times like these, our hearts can be so full that we especially welcome a little help with expressing our thoughts, prayers, and wishes. May this selection of prayers bless you and your loved ones as you prepare to honor those special occasions in life.

BAPTISM

Grant, O Lord, that as we are baptized into the death
of Your blessed Son, our Savior Jesus Christ,
so may we be buried with Him;
and that through the grave and gate of death,
we may pass to our joyful resurrection;
for His merits, who died, and was buried, and rose again
for us,
Your Son Jesus Christ our Lord.
—BOOK OF COMMON PRAYER

I take God the Father to be my God.
I take God the Son to be my Savior.
I take the Holy Ghost to be my Sanctifier.
I take the Word of God to be my rule;
I take the people of God to be my people;
And I do hereby dedicate and yield my whole self to
the Lord;
And I do this deliberately, freely, and forever.
—MATTHEW HENRY (1662–1714), ADAPTED

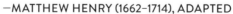

Heavenly Father, we praise You for this sacred moment,
for uniting us with Christ through baptism.
Thank You for cleansing us from our sin
and adopting us as Your own children!
Fill us with Your Holy Spirit and lead us in Your truth.
Help us to follow the way of Jesus,
to walk in Your love,
and to bless others with Your light.

—C. M.

Almighty God,
by our baptism into the death and resurrection
of Your Son Jesus Christ,
You turn us from the old life of sin.
Grant that we, being reborn to new life in Him,
may live in righteousness and holiness all our days;
through Jesus Christ our Lord,
who lives and reigns with You and the Holy Spirit,
one God,
now and forever.

—BOOK OF COMMON PRAYER

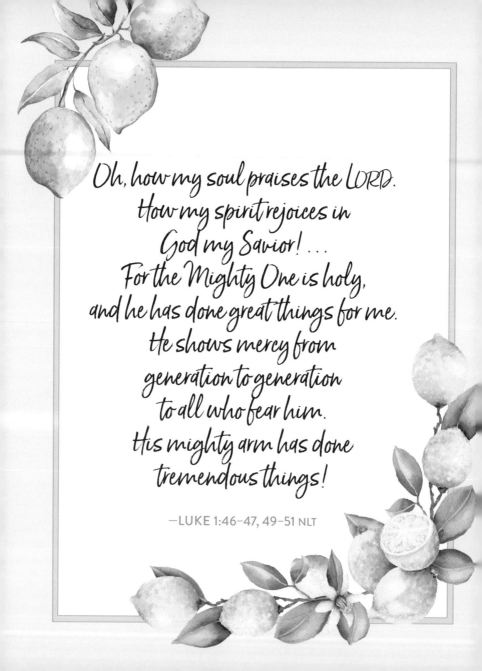

Oh, how my soul praises the LORD.
How my spirit rejoices in
God my Savior! ...
For the Mighty One is holy,
and he has done great things for me.
He shows mercy from
generation to generation
to all who fear him.
His mighty arm has done
tremendous things!

—LUKE 1:46–47, 49–51 NLT

BIRTH OF A BABY

O Lord my God,
shed the light of Your love on my child.
Keep him safe from all illness and all injury.
Enter his tiny soul,
and comfort him with Your peace and joy.
Let him as a child learn the way of your commandments.
As an adult let him live the full span of life,
serving Your kingdom on earth.
And finally in his old age, let him die in the sure
and certain knowledge of Your salvation.
Dear Lord, smile upon him.

   —JOHANN FRIEDRICH STARCK (1680–1756)

Into Your hands, O God, we place Your child _____.
Support him in his successes and failures,
in his joys and sorrows.
As he grows in age, may he grow in grace
and in the knowledge of his Savior Jesus Christ.

   —BOOK OF COMMON PRAYER

Lord, I praise You for this wonder before me,
this lovely and precious little person You have made
and brought into the world.
I am unspeakably humbled and honored
to participate in Your act of creation.
I thank You for this dear creature
to hold and cherish and nurture.
Give me the wisdom to discern this child's needs,
the will and ability to meet them,
and the grace to do so with Your character in me.

—C. M.

Almighty God, heavenly Father,
You have blessed us with the joy and care of children.
Help us have a lively sense of Your presence with us,
And give us calm strength and patient wisdom
as we bring them up,
that we may teach them to love
whatever is just and true and good,
following the example of our Savior Jesus Christ.

—BOOK OF COMMON PRAYER

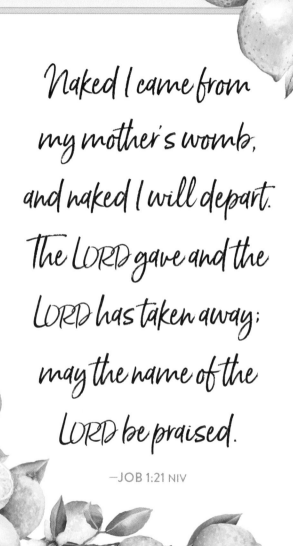

Naked I came from my mother's womb, and naked I will depart. The LORD gave and the LORD has taken away; may the name of the LORD be praised.

—JOB 1:21 NIV

DEATH OF A LOVED ONE

We give back to You, O God,
those whom You gave to us. . . .
Your Son has taught us that life is eternal
and love cannot die.
So death is only a horizon,
and a horizon is only the limit of our sight. . . .
You have told us that You are preparing a place for us:
prepare us, that where You are we may always be,
O dear Lord of life and death.

—WILLIAM PENN (1644–1718)

Go forth, O Christian soul, upon your journey from this
      world;
go in the name of God the Father who created you;
go in the mercy of Jesus, the Redeemer, who suffered for you;
go in the power of the Holy Spirit who was poured out
      for you.
In communion with the angels and saints,
may you be given eternal peace
and rest for ever in the presence of God.

—COMMENDATION OF A SOUL,
WESTERN RITE (ADAPTED)

Lord, You know how much we hurt
as we miss our loved ones.
You bear our grief with us
and accept us into Your compassionate care
as we feel so many things so intensely.
Help us remember You are still Lord and Father.
Help us think of death not only as a great tragedy
but also as a doorway to Your blessings and joy.
Give us peace as we think of the peace
You give our loved ones
who have passed into Your presence.
Give us hope that one day,
when we ourselves are redeemed from death and pain,
we will see them again.
They will be well—vibrant and strong in Your glory—
and we will know the sweetness of a reunion
in a place where all is new and perfect.
And together we will be fully alive in
Your love and power,
sharing in the all-surpassing delights of Your presence,
the joy of worship,
and all the beauty and gifts of heaven.

—C. M.

O Death, where is your sting? . . .
Christ is risen, and you are abolished! . . .
Christ is risen, and the angels rejoice.
Christ is risen, and the life reigns. . . .
For Christ, who rose from the dead,
has become the leader and the reviver
of those who have fallen asleep.
To Him be glory and dominion unto ages of ages!
—ST. JOHN CHRYSOSTOM (C. 347–407)

Lord Jesus, we praise You that You conquered death—
    death was swallowed up in victory!
You, the God of power and love, trampled down the barrier
between us and the Father of life and light,
overcoming the darkness,
defeating our sin and the enemy of our souls.
We thank You for the victory over sin and death
You give us through our union with You.
You make us conquerors through Your love.
We thank You that You promise
to transform our bodies
into new bodies that will never die,
and to bring us to our adoptive Father's home of blessings,
a bright new world of life and beauty and joy.
                        —C. M.

Lord, it belongs not to my care
Whether I die or live;
To love and serve You is my share,
And this Your grace must give.
If life be long, I will be glad,
That I may long obey;
If short, yet why should I be sad
To welcome endless day?
Christ leads me through no darker rooms
Than He went through before;
He that unto God's kingdom comes
Must enter by this door.
Come, Lord, when grace has made me meet
Your blessed face to see;
For if Your work on earth be sweet
What will Your glory be!
Then I shall end my sad complaints
And weary sinful days,
And join with the triumphant saints
That sing my Savior's praise.
My knowledge of that life is small,
The eye of faith is dim;
But 'tis enough that Christ knows all,
And I will be with Him.

—RICHARD BAXTER (1615–1691)

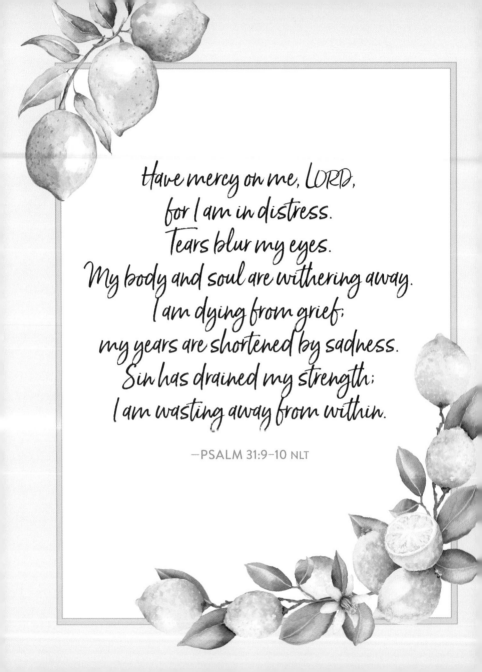

Have mercy on me, LORD,
for I am in distress.
Tears blur my eyes.
My body and soul are withering away.
I am dying from grief;
my years are shortened by sadness.
Sin has drained my strength;
I am wasting away from within.

—PSALM 31:9–10 NLT

GRADUATION

We give You thanks,
yes more than thanks, O Lord our God, . . .
for all Your goodness
at all times and in all places,
because You have shielded, rescued, helped,
and guided us all the days of our lives,
and brought us to this hour.
                    —LITURGY OF ST. JAMES

Lord, I am grateful for Your kindness to me:
          for helping me rise to challenges,
          navigate difficulties,
          grow through striving,
          and persevere to the finish line.
Thank You for every wise teacher and encouraging peer,
every stimulating lesson and interesting task.
Thank You for teaching me and building me up
through these people and experiences.
May what I have learned enable me to serve You
and bless others in new ways.
                    —C. M.

Gracious and loving God, . . .
I thank You for Your active presence in my busy life;
for the opportunities given, and the blessings received.
As I embrace the new season ahead . . . ,
breathe freely through me
and renew my spirit with fresh resolve and purpose.
Give me grace to be a good steward of all that You have
      entrusted to me.
Give me grace to serve You with a generous,
      compassionate, and loving heart. . . .
Give me the courage to be faithful.

        —ANONYMOUS

Send wisdom from Your throne of might,
to be with me,
to work with me,
to act in me,
to speak in me,
to order all my thoughts and words and deeds and
      plans
according to Your will and to the glory of Your name.

        —AELRED OF RIEVAULX (1109–1167)

Lord, thank You for the gifts of education and
    transformation;
      for learning communities and enriching
        experiences;
      for the family and friends who have supported me;
      for all the resources I needed to reach this point in
        my formation.
    Thank You for shaping me into someone new,
      for giving me a new capacity to serve and be an
        agent of change in this world.
Lead me into the good works You've prepared for me.
Bring my abilities and energy to where there is need.
Take me where You are working and use me to
    accomplish Your will.
May I do all things in love and with excellence.
        —C. M.

You are never tired, O Lord, of doing us good.
Let us never be weary of doing You service.
But as You have pleasure in the well-being of Your
    servants,
let us take pleasure in the service of our Lord
and abound in Your work and in Your love and praise
    evermore.
        —JOHN WESLEY (1703–1791)

WEDDING / ANNIVERSARY

The Lord sanctify and bless You,
the Lord pour the riches of His grace upon You,
that you may please Him
and live together in holy love
to your lives' end.

—JOHN KNOX (1513–1572)

O God, You have so consecrated the covenant of
      marriage
that in it is represented
the spiritual unity between Christ and His Church:
Send therefore Your blessing upon these Your servants,
that they may so love, honor, and cherish each other
in faithfulness and patience,
in wisdom and true godliness,
that their home may be a haven of blessing and peace.

—BOOK OF COMMON PRAYER

God, with Your grace,
help this man and woman:
that with true fidelity and steadfast love
they may honor and keep
the promises and vows they make. . . .
Give them wisdom and devotion
in the ordering of their
common life,
that each may be to the other
a strength in need,
a counselor in perplexity,
a comfort in sorrow,
and a companion in joy.
Grant that their wills may be so
knit together in Your will,
and their spirits in Your Spirit,
that they may grow in love and peace
with You and one another
all the days of their life. . . .
Give them grace,
when they hurt each other,
to recognize and acknowledge their fault,
and to seek each other's forgiveness
and Yours.

—BOOK OF COMMON PRAYER

Lord, we are grateful to experience You
through the holy gift of marriage.
May we daily honor the oaths we made
before You and unto You.
Help us never grow weary
of treating this sacred union with respect
and handling one another with the utmost care.
May we cherish belonging to each other and to You;
may we bless each other and be blessed by You.
Throughout every high and low place of life,
every thrill and sorrow,
every sweetness and strain,
unite us and bind us together in Your Spirit more
　　　and more.
May our attachment, devotion, and joy
grow and deepen
every day and every year.
Help us treat the gift of love as precious,
treasure each other,
and find ways to cause the other to feel treasured.

—C. M.

Thank You, Lord, for Your faithfulness to us
to help us be faithful to each other!
Thank You for the life we've built together—
our children and friendships,
our sweet rituals and laughter,
our home full of energy and personality,
all the life and joy of our little world.
Thank You for our bond of togetherness,
which serves both as a refuge
and a launching pad into the wider world to glorify You.
Preserve and protect who we are
and what we have invested in.
Lead us in growing into what You want us to become.
Continually build us up so we may be ever more fruitful
        for You.

—C. M.

May the Holy Spirit fill you both
with the immense, unending love of God.
May He guide you in wisdom and grace,
grant you patience and understanding,
and sustain you as you nurture each other.
May He lead you in fulfilling
your kingdom purposes as a couple.

—C. M.

Eight
Prayers for God's Will

The will of God prevails.
—ABRAHAM LINCOLN

*P*raying for God's will to be done is deceiving in its simplicity. We just talk (not unlike how we talk about what to have for dinner) . . . but as we're connecting with the One on the throne of the universe, our words carry the enormity of otherworldly, kingdom-of-heaven power.

Prayer is the equivalent of hurling a stone at a giant and knocking him down, or lifting up a walking stick that parts the Red Sea. These actions of faith say, "This is what the Almighty has ordained; so it shall be. What I'm doing is part of what He's doing."

As we submit to God, walk closely with Him, and become like Him, we have the honor of not only participating in His divine nature but also partnering in His work.

As temples of God housing His Spirit, we take on the mind of Christ, along with His desires and loves, and align our will with His. We cooperate with Him in pronouncing what is right and good and what ought to be.

We promote peace, call for justice, bring healing, and make room for God's order, harmony, and joy. We bring His kingdom of light and freedom. The world around us should change because of our prayers.

Through prayer, we express love to our family and friends well by ushering into their lives the very best thing they could receive: God's goodness and blessings. We are like the men who carried their paralyzed friend to Jesus, lowering him through a roof to receive a miracle and be healed. We prove our faith in Jesus' power and take part in showing the entire world just how beautiful and amazing He is.

Aligning our wills with God's will also means praying for God's help and wisdom to do our individual part in His big-picture agenda. We are called to take ownership for the areas in which we need to grow. We want to "make every effort" to add more godly character qualities to our faith, which will keep us from "being ineffective and unproductive" in our knowledge of Christ (2 Peter 1:5-8 NIV).

We surrender ourselves to Him, willing to be molded and dependent on His transforming Spirit. And as He changes us, we become agents of change for His glory.

YOUR MARRIAGE

Father, may nothing cause unkindness between us—
no mistake or discontentment,
no distrust or sorrow.
May we so dearly and loyally attend
to each other's good and contentment,
that we may always please You.
Through this may we learn and practice
our duty and greatest love to You,
and become mutual helps to each other
as we grow in godliness.
After we have received the blessings of a married life—
the comforts of fellowship,
the endearments of a holy and great affection,
the blessing of children—
may we forever dwell together
in the embraces of Your love and glories,
feasting in the marriage supper of the Lamb to
eternal ages.
—JEREMY TAYLOR (1613–1667),
ADAPTED

Lord, pour Your goodness into our marriage.
Shape our relationship with Your power and love.
Free us from resentment, self-righteousness,
and stubbornness,
from anything that cools our affection,
pushes us apart, or hardens our hearts.
When we feel distant or hurt,
when we struggle to trust or forgive or engage,
come and overpower us with Your love.
Make us brave to initiate connection and affection,
to be open and risk vulnerability,
to give compassion and kindness.
Make us quick to turn to the other,
to listen and acknowledge,
to lift them up
and put their needs and feelings above our own.
Prune away our selfishness, Lord.
Help us learn the meaning of love together.
Heal our wounds and soften our hearts.
Transform us with Your grace.
Help us strengthen our commitment to each other
and put energy into building *us*.
Lead us into deeper joys of intimacy,
of knowing each other better all the time,
and of growing together.

—C. M.

May your fountain be blessed,
and may you rejoice in the
wife of your youth.

—PROVERBS 5:18 NIV

Lord, in our marriage,
help us show each other Your heart—
a heart of unconditional, exuberant love,
of earnest loyalty,
of compassion and grace that never run out,
of tenderness and affection.
May we have a spirit of
rejoicing over the other with singing.
May my behavior show my spouse that . . .

> I am *for* them;
> I am their biggest supporter;
> I have relentless belief in their abilities and
> purpose;
> I celebrate and delight in who they are,
> exactly as You have made them;

I feel privileged to be on this journey of growth
with them.
May I never stop trying to build our bond
and make them feel my love.
Help us stand strong in Your truth and
be full of hope and courage,
ready to tackle challenges
and face all of life together in Your Spirit.

—C. M.

In our marriage,
may the faithful life of Christ be our vision—
His humility our goal,
His loyal devotion our aim,
His sacrificial love our guide,
His joyful service our example.

—C. M.

Make our life together a sign of Christ's love
to this sinful and broken world,
that unity may overcome estrangement,
forgiveness heal guilt,
and joy conquer despair.

—BOOK OF COMMON PRAYER

May the words of our mouths,
the meditations of our hearts,
our choices in private moments,
and the way we treat each other
be pleasing to You, O Lord, our Rock and Redeemer.

—C. M.

YOUR FAMILY AND FRIENDS

God our Father,
You see Your children growing up
in an unsteady and confusing world.
Show them that Your ways
give more life than the ways of the world,
and that following You
is better than chasing after selfish goals.
Help them to take failure
not as a measure of their worth,
but as a chance for a new start.
Give them strength to hold their faith in You
and to keep alive their joy in Your creation.
—BOOK OF COMMON PRAYER

Inspire and strengthen us by Your Holy Spirit, O
    Lord God,
to seek Your will and uphold Your honor in all things;
in the purity and joy of our homes,
in the trust and fellowship of our common life,
in daily service of the good;
after the pattern and in the power
of Your Son, our Lord and Savior, Jesus Christ.
—JEREMY TAYLOR (1613–1667)

Almighty God,
You set the solitary in families.
We offer them up to You for Your continual care.
Remove every root of bitterness,
self-righteousness,
and pride in us.
Fill us with faith, virtue, knowledge,
self-control, patience, and godliness.
Knit together in constant affection those
who have been united in holy wedlock.
Turn the hearts of parents to children,
and the hearts of children to parents;
and so enkindle empathy and grace among us all,
that we may evermore be devoted to one another
and be bonded in love.

    —BOOK OF COMMON PRAYER, ADAPTED

O God, make the door of this house wide enough
to receive all who need human love and friendship,
but narrow enough to shut out all envy, pride, and malice.
Make its threshold smooth enough
to be no stumbling block to children,
nor to straying feet,
but strong enough to turn away the power of evil.
God, make the door of this house
a gateway to Your eternal kingdom.

    —THOMAS KEN (1637–1711), ADAPTED

Bless and sanctify our home—
those who live in it and everything in it. . . .
Fill it with all good things.
Grant us an abundance of blessings from heaven
and the substance of life from the richness of the earth.
Direct the longings of our prayers to the fruits of Your mercy. . . .
May Your angels of light live within the walls of this house
and guard all who live in it.

   —CATHOLIC PRAYER

Be gracious to all who are near and dear to me
and keep us all in Your love.
Guide us, good Lord, and govern us by the same Spirit,
that we may be so united to You here on earth
that we will not be divided when You call us home.

   —JOHN WESLEY (1703–1791), ADAPTED

Make Your love our love.
Make Your joy our joy.
Make Your peace our peace.
May Your kindness and generosity permeate our relationships.
May Your humility and patience guide every interaction.
May Your grace shape our way of life.

   —C. M.

Almighty God, and most merciful Father,
You have given us a new command that we should love
    one another;
give us also grace that we may fulfill it.
Make us gentle and kind, bearing with one another.
May we each look to the good of the other in word and deed.
We offer our friendships for Your holy use, by the blessing
    of Your Spirit.
—BROOKE FOSS WESTCOTT (1825–1901), ADAPTED

May we throw off every hindrance to love.
Father, You are the giver of every good gift,
including laughter.
Help us see the humor in our everyday life
and be willing to laugh at ourselves.
May we notice the small things
that make us happy or chuckle
and hold on to that cheer.
May moments of levity lift us up
and steer us away from irritability and pessimism,
complaints and grudges.
Bring us Your freedom and lightness,
and fill our hearts with Your love and joy.
Help us keep choosing to make our life sweet and merry.
—C. M.

Jesus, lead me in loving others
the way You have loved me.
You say real love is giving up Your own life
for Your friends;
show me how You want me to give of myself.
Help me prioritize others' needs
and put aside my own desires
in order to bless and care for them.

—C. M.

YOUR COMMUNITY

O Lord, save us from self-centeredness in our prayers,
and help us to remember to pray for others.
May we be so lovingly absorbed with those for whom
    we pray
that we may feel their needs as keenly as our own,
and intercede for them sensitively,
with understanding and imagination.

—JOHN CALVIN (1509–1564), ADAPTED

Help me make my community better
and bring any change I hope to see.
Make me bold in taking initiative
to serve others and meet needs,
to bring cheer and lift spirits,
to brighten the lives of those around me.
May my acts of kindness show others Your love
and draw them closer to You.

—C. M.

Give us more charity,
more self-denial,
more likeness to You.
Teach us to sacrifice our comforts to others,
and our likings for the sake of doing good.
Make us kind in thought,
gentle in word,
generous in deed.
Teach us that it is better to give than to receive;
better to forget ourselves than to put ourselves forward;
better to minister than to be ministered unto.
And unto You, the God of love,
be all the glory and praise,
both now and forevermore.

—HENRY ALFORD (1810–1871)

O God You have bound us together in a common life.
Help us, in the midst of our struggles for justice and
    truth,
to confront one another without hatred or bitterness,
and to work together with patience and respect.
    —BOOK OF COMMON PRAYER, ADAPTED

Keep us, O God, from all pettiness,
let us be large in thought, in word, in deed.
Let us be done with the fault finding
and leave off all self-seeking.
May we put away all pretense
and meet each other face-to-face
without self-pity and without prejudice.
May we never be hasty in judgment and always generous.
Let us take time for all things,
and make us grow calm, serene, and gentle.
Teach us to put into action our better impulses,
straightforward and unafraid.
Grant that we may realize
that it is the little things of life that create differences,
that in the big things of life, we are as one.
And, O Lord God, let us not forget to be kind!
    —MARY STUART,
      QUEEN OF SCOTLAND (1542–1587)

Lord, help us take care of the weak and needy,
and encourage those who are timid or troubled.
May we be considerate and gracious,
patiently bearing with one another
and being good to each other
for Your sake.

—C. M.

Pour into our hearts the spirit of unselfishness,
so that, when our cup overflows,
we may seek to share our happiness with others.
O God of love,
who makes the sun to rise on the evil and on the good,
who sends rain on the just and the unjust,
grant that we may become more and more Your true
   children
by receiving into our souls more of Your own spirit
of ungrudging and unwearying kindness.

—JOHN HUNTER (1849–1917)

Father, help us to see with Your eyes
the needs of the people around us.

—C. M.

Watch, dear Lord, with those who wake or weep tonight,
and let Your angels protect those who sleep.
Tend the sick.
Refresh the weary.
Sustain the dying.
Calm the suffering.
Pity the distressed.
Shield the joyous.
We ask this for Your love's sake.

—ST. AUGUSTINE OF HIPPO (354–430)

THE CHURCH

Lord, we pray for the unity of Your Church.
Help us to see ourselves as rays from the one sun,
branches of a single tree,
and streams flowing from one river.
May we remain united to You and to each other,
because You are our common source of life.
May we send out Your light
and pour forth Your flowing streams over all the earth,
drawing our inspiration and joy from You.

—ST. CYPRIAN OF CARTHAGE (C. 200–258),

ADAPTED

Lord, help us be faithful.
We want to please You and glorify You!
May we prove to the world
we are Your disciples
by the way we love.
May we devote our energy
to fulfilling our mission,
bringing people to Your grace
and into a life of worship.
May we handle Your Word rightly
and share Your life-giving gospel.
May we offer our whole selves to You
as a sacrifice of praise,
as a joyful surrender to our good King.
May we depend on and yield
to Your Spirit of truth,
our Helper and Guide,
in all things and at all times.
May we treasure You most and seek You first.
May we put You on display, Lord,
showing Your truth, love, peace, joy, and glory
every way we can.

—C. M.

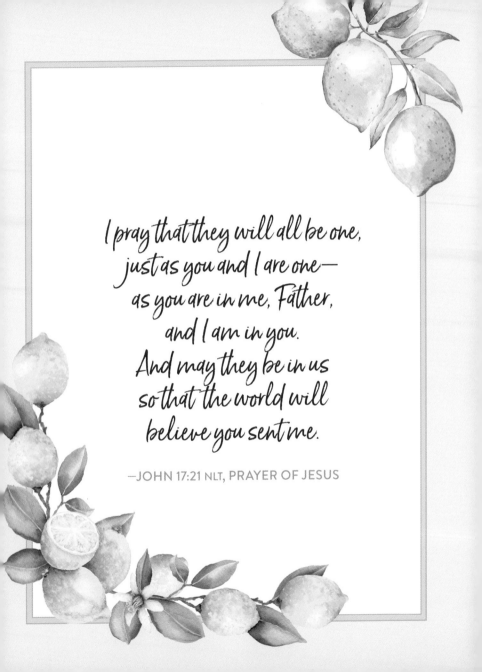

I pray that they will all be one,
just as you and I are one—
as you are in me, Father,
and I am in you.
And may they be in us
so that the world will
believe you sent me.

—JOHN 17:21 NLT, PRAYER OF JESUS

Lord and Master of our lives,
take from us the spirit of laziness,
half-heartedness,
selfish ambition,
and idle talk.
Give us rather the spirit of integrity,
purity of heart,
humility,
faithfulness,
and love.
Lord and King, help us to see our own errors,
and not to judge our neighbors;
for Your mercy's sake.

—ORTHODOX LITURGY, ADAPTED

God bless this church and parish,
and prosper all our attempts to be faithful
and to draw others to You,
for Jesus Christ's sake.

—OLD SCOTTISH PRAYER

O God the Father of our Lord Jesus Christ,
the Prince of Peace, . . .
Take away all hatred and prejudice,
and whatever else may hinder us
from godly union and harmony.
There is only one Body and one Spirit,
one hope of our calling,
one Lord, one Faith, one Baptism,
one God and Father of us all.
So may we be of one heart and one soul,
united in one holy bond of truth, peace, faith, and
    charity.
May we, with one mind and one mouth, glorify You. . . .
Almighty Father,
whose blessed Son before His passion
prayed for His disciples that they might be one,
even as You and He are one:
Grant that Your Church,
being bound together in love and obedience to You,
may be united in one body by the one Spirit,
that the world may believe in Him whom You sent.

    —BOOK OF COMMON PRAYER, ADAPTED

LEADERS

Almighty God, only You have eternal power.
Any human power is borrowed from You.
May all those with authority
use it for good and to honor You.

    —WILLIAM TYNDALE (1494–1536), ADAPTED

O righteous Lord, You love righteousness.
May Your Holy Spirit be with our rulers,
that they may govern in faith and honor,
striving to put down all that is evil
and encourage all that is good.
Give Your spirit of wisdom to lawmakers.
May they grasp the gravity of the work
You have given them to do,
that they may not do it lightly.
May they put away all wrong and oppression
and advance the welfare of all people.

    —THOMAS ARNOLD (1795–1842), ADAPTED

God, reveal Yourself to those
who have power in this world.
Help them behold Your glory
and humble themselves before You.
Build their faith in You;
grow their love for Your ways
and grow their love for the people they represent.
Give them wisdom and discernment;
make them pure-hearted, respectful, diligent, and
    conscientious.
Save them from selfishness, pride, corruption, and
    hardheartedness.
May they honor You
by honoring those they serve,
treating them with dignity and kindness.
May they lead with prudence and love,
cultivating justice and mercy.
Help them persevere
in doing what is right in Your eyes,
both privately and publicly.
Bless and help these stewards of great responsibility,
    Lord.
Weave them into Your kingdom work
and use them to carry out Your purposes.

—C. M.

O Lord our Governor,
bless the leaders of our land,
that we may be a people at peace among ourselves
and a blessing to other nations of the earth.
Lord, keep this nation under Your care. . . .
Send down upon those who hold office
the spirit of wisdom, charity, and justice;
that with steadfast purpose
they may faithfully serve in their offices
to promote the well-being of all people.
—BOOK OF COMMON PRAYER

Almighty God,
all thoughts of truth and peace proceed from You.
Kindle in the hearts of all people
the true love of peace.
Guide every leader in every nation
in Your pure and peaceable wisdom,
so that Your kingdom may go forward,
till the whole earth is filled
with the knowledge of Your love.
—FRANCIS PAGET (1851–1911), ADAPTED

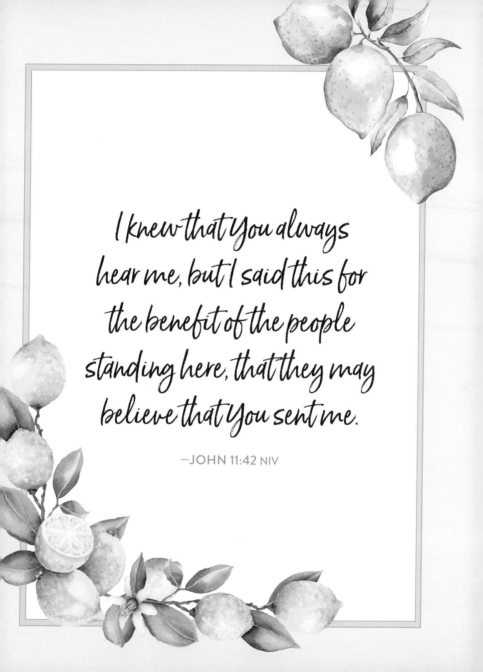

I knew that You always hear me, but I said this for the benefit of the people standing here, that they may believe that You sent me.

—JOHN 11:42 NIV

THE WORLD

Almighty God,
in giving us dominion over things on earth,
You made us fellow workers in Your creation.
Give us wisdom and reverence
to use the resources of nature
so that no one may suffer from our abuse of them,
and that generations to come
may continue to praise You for Your bounty.
        —BOOK OF COMMON PRAYER

God of love, whose compassion never fails,
we bring before You the troubles and perils
of people and nations—
the sighing of prisoners and captives,
the sorrows of the bereaved,
the needs of strangers,
the helplessness of the weak,
the despondency of the weary,
the failing powers of the aged.
O Lord, draw near to each.
        —ST. ANSELM OF CANTERBURY (1033–1109)

O God,
You are the author of love,
and You love pure peace and affection.
Heal the diseases of all . . . who are sick,
and in Your great mercy set free
all who are terrified by fears,
afflicted by poverty,
weary with trouble,
worn down by illness,
burdened with punishment,
and all prisoners and wanderers.
Show them Your compassion daily,
lift them up . . . and protect them.

—GALLICAN SACRAMENTARY

Look in compassion, O heavenly Father,
upon this troubled and divided world.
Though we cannot trace Your footsteps
or understand Your working,
give us grace to trust You.
And when the time is right,
reveal Your new heaven and earth,
where Your people will live
and where the Prince of Peace rules.

—CHARLES JOHN VAUGHAN (1816–1897), ADAPTED

We beg You, Lord, to help and defend us.
Deliver the oppressed, . . .
raise the fallen,
show Yourself to the needy,
heal the sick,
bring back those of Your people who have gone astray,
feed the hungry,
lift up the weak,
take off the prisoners' chains.
May every nation come to know that You alone are God,
that Jesus Christ is Your Son,
and that we are Your people, the sheep of Your pasture.
—ST. CLEMENT OF ROME (C. 35–99)

Almighty God,
you have created us in your own image.
Grant us grace to contend against evil fearlessly
and to fight against oppression.
May we use our freedom reverently,
bringing justice to our communities
and among the nations,
to the glory of your holy name.
—BOOK OF COMMON PRAYER, ADAPTED

Father God, bring Your kingdom into our hearts,
into our families and communities,
into the nations throughout the world.
Make Your purposes our purposes.
Make Your agenda our agenda.
Take us into the trenches of Your work.
Show us how we can bring peace and justice,
and help people flourish.
Draw people to Yourself through us.
May our actions cause them to honor and delight in You.
Lead us in serving in the name of Jesus
and redeeming the brokenness of this world.
Give us courage and strength to persevere.
May we count it a great privilege and joy
to spend ourselves for the good of others
and for Your glory.

—C. M.

Heavenly Father, may Your Holy Spirit lead
the rich nations to support the poor,
and the strong nations to protect the weak,
so that every nation may develop in its own way
and work together with other nations in true partnership
for the promotion of peace and the good of all people.

—ANONYMOUS

Nine

Prayers of Blessing and Encouragement for Others

How blessings brighten as they take their flight.
—EDWARD YOUNG

The last thing Jesus did before He ascended into heaven was something He had done frequently throughout His ministry: "He lifted up his hands and blessed" people (Luke 24:50 NIV).

When we bless others in Jesus' name, we are linking them with the power and life of God. It's as though we are lifting them up out of a shadow and into the bright rays of God's light, full of His goodness and glory. We are putting them in the Father's care, securing them in the shelter of His love.

Prayer is a work of ministry; it should be a normal part of daily life in the body of Christ. With the Spirit at work through the different members, we encourage one another by reminding each other what is true. First Thessalonians 5:11 tells us, "Encourage one another and build each other up" (NIV). Prayer is one more way we can build each other up and spur one another on toward faith-filled living. We are strengthened by hoping and standing in faith together.

We give those who are especially struggling new courage by linking arms with them and standing with them in life-changing realities: that nothing is impossible for God, His presence is with us, and heaven is our future. As we do so, we're throwing open the windows of their souls, bringing in fresh air to revitalize them.

As we bless and encourage and build up, we experience the privilege of continuing Jesus' practice as well as the joy of taking part in the good things He wants to do for the people around us.

Perhaps you already regularly say prayers of blessing and encouragement for certain people in your life. As you read over these selections of prayers, notice if God puts someone else on your heart to pray for.

Fair warning: as you pray for God to bless the people in your life, He may call *you* to be the one to bring those blessings on His behalf. After all, prayer is a two-way conversation. While praying, you may hear a still, small voice urging you to act—offering you an opportunity to reach out to that person directly, beyond simply praying for them. When this happens, it's exciting to see that God is alive and active in our lives.

God, our great Protector,
watch over these dear ones I love.
Be with them through every step they take,
shielding, guiding, and strengthening them.
Keep them in Your love.
God, our great Provider,
open Your hand and give them exactly what they need—
nourish their souls, minds, and bodies.
Make them healthy and vibrant,
ready for their next steps with You—
the next challenge, adventure, important work,
or good surprise You have in store for them.
God, our good King,
we take joy in belonging to You
and put all our trust in You.

—C. M.

May God the Father who made us bless us.
May God the Son send His healing among us.
May God the Holy Spirit move within us
and give us eyes to see with,
ears to hear with,
and hands that Your work might be done.
May we walk and preach the word of God to all.
May the angel of peace watch over us
and lead us at last by God's grace to His kingdom.

—ST. DOMINIC (1170–1221)

May you remember your great value to God
and His purpose for you in this world:

> to know, enjoy, and worship Him;
> to become like Him;
> and to join Him in His work
> of bringing His goodness, love, and life to
> people.

May you rejoice in the privilege of belonging to Him
and fulfilling the good works He's prepared for you in
His kingdom.

May you rest in the knowledge that you yourself are
God's handiwork;

> that even now His mighty power is at work
> within you,
> and that He will continue working
> until He completes what He has started.

—C. M.

Almighty God,
we entrust all who are dear to us
to Your never-failing care and love,
for this life and the life to come,
knowing that You are doing for them
better things than we can desire or pray for,
through Jesus Christ our Lord.

—BOOK OF COMMON PRAYER

Peace to this house from God our heavenly Father.
Peace to this house from His Son who is our peace.
Peace to this house from the Holy Spirit the
    Life-giver.
And the peace of the Lord be always with you.

—TRADITIONAL

May you draw close to Him who
came from heaven to earth to save you;
chose you to become His child;
knows you best;
loves you most;
and promises never to leave you.
May He help you and take care of you in every way.
May His Spirit infuse your heart
and your life with His bright beauty:
        love, joy, peace, patience, kindness, goodness,
        faithfulness, gentleness, and self-control;
        courage, strength, resilience, perseverance,
        faith, hope, and purity.
May His extravagant love,
abundant joy,
and overflowing grace
in your life bless others around you.

—C. M.

May God grow you and delight you
as you come to know Him more
and experience Him more deeply.
May He lead you in living a life that honors Him.
May He give you spiritual wisdom
and produce in you every kind of good fruit.
Through His immeasurable power
may He strengthen you with all the endurance
and patience you'll need.
May the Spirit lead you
to rehearse His amazing works
and to revel in His great rescue of your soul,
pulling you from darkness to light.
May your joy spill out into praise
as you realize the abundance of the life
He's brought you into,
the inheritance He's given you,
and the bright future He's prepared for you.

—C. M.

May God the Father bless us,
may Christ take care of us,
the Holy Ghost enlighten us all the days of our lives.
The Lord be our defender and keeper of body and soul,
both now and forever, to the ages of ages.

—ST. ETHELWOLD OF WINCHESTER (909–984)

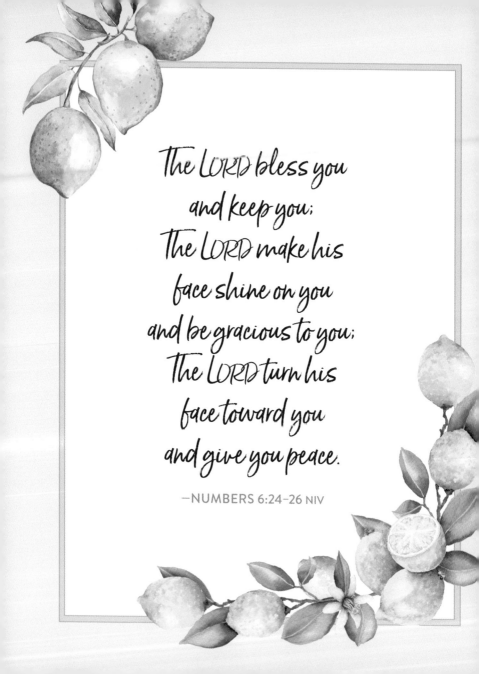

The LORD bless you
and keep you;
The LORD make his
face shine on you
and be gracious to you;
The LORD turn his
face toward you
and give you peace.

—NUMBERS 6:24–26 NIV